T0381173

I finished the devotional Discovering Jesus this morning. Yes, it is theologically accurate. I would expect nothing less from you. But it is the way you write it that captures me. Always grounded in scripture, always glorifying Jesus, always dripping with grace. This is written from the heart and hand of a dear man that knows the pain of brokenness and the joy of worship and the peace of being held close to the chest of the Father. My friend, I hear your voice in the pages and once again I get to experience the soul of a brother I love and respect. This book was written with tears of suffering and worship and love for Jesus. I look forward to having a bound copy in my hand and giving it away to friends and family.

Dr. Harrison Spitler
Pastor of Leadership Development and Shepherding
Hilton Head Presbyterian Church

Daniel's love for Christ and passion for others to know our savior shines through in Discovering Jesus. Each daily reading combines depth of content with a warmth that has been seasoned by a life of service. You'll be challenged in your walk, encouraged by Christ's love, and reminded that in Christ are hidden all the treasures and wisdom of knowledge.

Rev Jeff Lee
Campus Minister for Reformed University Fellowship at FAU

Discovering Jesus

Finding the gospel in everyday life

DANIEL T. ROGERS

WESTBOW
PRESS®
A DIVISION OF THOMAS NELSON
& ZONDERVAN

WestBow Press books may be ordered through booksellers or by contacting:

WestBow Press
A Division of Thomas Nelson & Zondervan
1663 Liberty Drive
Bloomington, IN 47403
www.westbowpress.com
844-714-3454

ISBN: 979-8-3850-3041-5 (sc)
ISBN: 979-8-3850-3042-2 (hc)
ISBN: 979-8-3850-3043-9 (e)

Library of Congress Control Number: 2024916123

Print information available on the last page.

WestBow Press rev. date: 10/22/2024

To my grandchildren, discover Christ. There is nothing else of comparison or value.

Contents

Introduction

About ten years ago, I began writing a devotional for the youth at Christ Our Hope Church in Wake Forest, North Carolina. I was serving as a ruling elder at the church, and as part of that role, I led the youth program. During one of the semesters, I determined to walk through the book of Mark with the students under the title of "Discovering Jesus." To aid them in this, I provided them with a fifty-day devotional. This book you hold was born out of that devotional and incorporates occasional diversions to other areas of scripture that speak to what we see in Mark.

The book of Mark has always held a dear space in my heart. As someone who has struggled to read, I love its brevity, clarity, and swift-moving action. As you walk through Mark, you are quickly confronted with two narratives: who Jesus is and what he came to do. This is known as the person and work of Christ. That picture is what we will seek to discover together over the following pages.

On a personal note, I have been asked which passage of scripture means the most to me or what my life verse is. I hold four passages of scripture very dear.

1. Hebrews 2 sums up all of scripture in just a few verses.
2. Hebrews 13:26–29 reminds me that no matter what is happening around me, nothing can shake my King.
3. John 10:29 points to the security I have in Christ.
4. Mark 1:1 reminds me that in light of all eternity, all good news begins with Christ and I don't have to look any other place.

Over these next few pages, I pray you will discover Jesus. I pray you will come face-to-face with the King of Kings. When you do, you will never be the same. There is nothing of comparison or value to Jesus. He is truly enough, for his glory and his glory alone.

Christ Alone

The beginning of the gospel about Jesus Christ, the Son of God.
—Mark 1:1

Many things about Christianity offend the world, not the least of which is the exclusivity of the gospel. I am sure that the statement "Christ alone" offends. You can hear the objection, can't you? "Surely there are other paths to God. Christianity is just one of those paths," they argue. However, Jesus's reply was clear, "I am the way, the truth and the life. No one comes to the Father except through me" (John 14:6). The statement leaves no room for other paths, other options, or other religions. What Jesus articulates to his disciples at the end of his ministry could not be plainer: Christ alone serves as the hope of the world, offers salvation from sins, and represents the only path to heaven and eternal life. Christ alone.

Mark begins his gospel with the same proclamation, stating that in light of all eternity, all good news begins with Christ. Apart from him, there is no good news. The gospel begins and ends with him. The gospel is about him, owned by him, and offered by him. The implications of this are far-reaching. You see, if Jesus lied, then Christianity is a path to nowhere. However, if Christ was telling the truth, there is only one way.

He is the way, the truth, and the life. To be clear, he is the only way, the only truth, and the only life. Those who look anywhere else will only find darkness, disappointment, and despair. He alone

1

is the source of our good news. In him alone we must trust. Christ alone. The road of life offers many paths and goes many places. But only one leads to redemption. Only one path offers life abundant, filled with purpose, hope, and direction. Only one path grants grace, mercy, forgiveness, and restoration. Only one path seeks social justice and selfless living.

On the Mount of Transfiguration, God the Father said, "This is my Son, whom I love. Listen to him!" (Mark 9:7). If we listen to him, we will hear what we need to know for eternal life, Christ alone. As you march down the road of life, listen to him (Ps. 119:105), acknowledge him (Prov. 3:6), believe him (1 John 3:23), trust him (Ps. 20:7–8), and share him (Rom. 10:15).

Hear the good news the gospel proclaims: Christ alone. In Christ alone, you will find joy in the journey, life abundant, purpose, and glory. Along life's journey, don't miss this point: Jesus is the Christ, the Messiah, the Savior, and the Son of the Living God. In all things, give him alone glory and honor.

The Gospel at the Start

But we see him who for a little while was made lower than the angels, namely Jesus, crowned with glory and honor because of the suffering of death, so that by the grace of God he might taste death for everyone.
—Hebrews 2:9

At the beginning of Hebrews 2, we have a picture of creation and the fall. Verse 8 leaves us with the image that things aren't right, that things aren't the way they should be. Then those words of good news in verse 9 appear, giving hope and offering redemption, "But we see Jesus," the great and mighty one who came to redeem what Adam lost. This is the beginning of the gospel of Jesus Christ. This is what Mark begins with. Our champion has come!

To be clear, the gospel doesn't mean that everything in this life will be perfect, sickness will cease, troubles will be no more, or poverty will turn to riches. No, the gospel has to do fundamentally with relationships—our relationship with God, ourselves, others, the world, and our work. The gospel, simply put, is that Jesus came to live the perfect life that we could not so he could pay the penalty for sin that we could not so he could rise again, ensuring our eternal life with him. The gospel represents a gracious gift, something we could never earn. The gospel comes to us by grace through faith in Christ, and it demands a response.

Hebrews 2 is one of my favorite passages in scripture. Why? It provides a picture of the gospel in just a few short breaths. We see our condition, what we have done. We see a Father who passionately

3

pursues us by not even sparing his Son. We see creation groaning under the weight of sin and oppression rejoicing at the coming redemption. We see redemption in our relationships, not just with God but also with others around us. We see that hatred can be turned to love, bitterness to forgiveness, despair to hope, injustice to justice, and disorder to order. We see Jesus coming into the midst of our mess and establishing his kingdom. That, too, is what Mark tells us at the beginning.

What does the gospel communicate to me?

1. Romans 8 tells me I am no longer held captive to the guilt and shame that shackled me to my sin—past, present, and future. These chains have been broken, shattered into a million pieces.
2. Galatians 5 tells me I now have a purpose for life beyond myself. In my freedom from sin, I am free to love, free to forgive, free to build, and free to live.
3. John 14 tells me I know who I am, where I came from, who sends me, and where I am going. I have a future that is secure in the one who conquered death.

So what is the gospel to me? It is everything. The stuff of this world has no hold. Death scares me no more. What then will I do with the gospel? I throw off everything that hinders and the sin that so easily entangles and with perseverance I run the race marked out for me, fixing my eyes on Jesus, the pioneer and perfecter of faith (Heb. 12:1–2). Rest in the gospel, dear reader. There is nothing of equal value or comparison to it.

No Other

You shall have no other gods before me.

—Exodus 20:3

The first of the Ten Commandments found in Exodus 20:3, "You shall have no other gods before me," should cause us to consider the practical application of what it means to live Christ alone in our lives. We can apply this commandment in one of two ways: sequentially or locationally.

First, the commandment could be applied sequentially. In other words, we would order the important things of life in a manner similar to the following: God, family, work, football, and so forth. Thinking sequentially allows us to have other gods as long as God comes first.

The problem with applying this command sequentially is that the purpose and object of our affection change with each god, allowing us to compartmentalize the one true God. The key question to understand whether to apply this command sequentially is simple: Would you ever come into the presence of your king flaunting another king?

Second, the commandment could be applied locationally. In other words, we would not be permitted to have any other gods before him or in his presence. If God is omnipresent, this would mean that we are to have no other gods but him, period. By applying this command locationally, the purpose and object of our affection remain the same, irrespective of what we do, God alone. Everything else on the list before God no longer appears. This doesn't mean the activities go away. Rather, the what, why, and how for each activity becomes singularly focused, God's glory alone.

God calls the Christian to locational living. There is no room for other gods in his presence. Scripture puts it this way, "So whether you eat or drink or whatever you do, do it all for the glory of God" (1 Cor. 10:31). To the most basic things of life—eating and drinking—we are to do all things for God's glory. If you are finding yourself living sequentially, give those things to God and make him the reason why you do what you do.

The Passionate Pursuit

As it is written in Isaiah the prophet: "I will send my messenger ahead of you, who will prepare your way"—"a voice of one calling in the desert, 'Prepare the way for the Lord, make straight paths for him.'"

—Mark 1:2–3

From the beginning of time, God the Father determined a plan for salvation; God the Son carried out the plan through his perfect life, substitutionary death, resurrection, and ascension; and God the Spirit made sure that God's children who were far off heard the good news and responded with faith. In the midst of his plan, God uses people to share the good news of the gospel. We see this clearly in Romans 10:13–15,

> "Everyone who calls on the name of the Lord will be saved." How, then, can they call on the one they have not believed in? And how can they believe in the one of whom they have not heard? And how can they hear without someone preaching to them? And how can anyone preach unless they are sent? As it is written: "How beautiful are the feet of those who bring good news!"

And so, John came to prepare the way for the coming Messiah. John declared that the promise of God had come in time and space to save his people from their sins. John called the people to repent and be baptized. Make straight paths, he said. It is easy to focus on this aspect of the prophecy and miss something truly profound, God's passionate pursuit of his children. This is what we see from Isaiah 40:4–5, "Every valley shall be raised up, every mountain and hill made low; the rough ground shall become level, the rugged places a plain. And the glory of the Lord will be revealed, and all people will see it together. For the mouth of the Lord has spoken."

God will not let anything get in the way of you seeing him. This he has promised; this he will carry out. The mountains will be squashed; the valleys will be raised up; the path will be cleared. All of this shouts rather loudly of a God who passionately loves you and pursues after you, sparing not even his only beloved Son to redeem you. In the midst of this, he sends people throughout your life who proclaim the gospel truth. One question remains: what will you do with what you hear? Joshua asked this of the people of Israel at the end of his life, "then choose for yourselves this day whom you will serve … But as for me and my household, we will serve the LORD" (Josh. 24:15).

As the people declared allegiance to God, he concluded by saying, "'Now then,' said Joshua, 'throw away the foreign gods that are among you and yield your hearts to the LORD, the God of Israel'" (Josh. 24:23).

Throw away the gods among you and become a part of his passionate pursuit. Clear the way, remove the impediments, and point others to Christ. There is no greater pursuit in life worth taking.

The Promise of the Prodigal

But while he was still a long way off, his father saw him and was filled with compassion for him; he ran to his son, threw his arms around him and kissed him.

—Luke 15:20

The story of the prodigal son has captivated readers for two thousand years. In it, we see a son come to his father, demand his inheritance, leave for a far-off land, and squander what was graciously given. We then see the son come to his senses, return home in humility, repent of his sins, and submit to the father's sentence. Finally, we see the son restored, a party thrown, and forgiveness granted. This picture of redemption and restoration gives hope to people who continually return time and again to the pigpens of life.

However, we must not overlook the prodigal son's father within the story, the one who provides the grace needed for redemption and restoration. In the story, we see the father who spends time looking for his son's return. We see a father who knows the footfall of his son before he even recognizes his face. We see a father who doesn't care about propriety in running out to greet his son who ran off. We see a father who spares no expense in welcoming back his son. We see a father who stands in the gap for the son when others would have him expel the prodigal. We see a father who loves his son beyond measure. We see a father who forgives beyond measure the sins of his son. We see a father passionate in his pursuit of his son.

The father in the story represents God. The prodigal son represents all those who would be called his people. Knowing this to be the case, practically speaking, how do we respond to the redemption and restoration offered freely by grace through faith? Will you continue to wallow in the pigpens of life making mud pies? Will you come home yet remain outside living as a hired hand? Or will you come home as a son and live in the midst of God's grace and forgiveness? I would encourage you to put away your pigpens and repent of the wayward life in a far-off land. I would encourage you to return home to find your heavenly Father ready to receive you as a son with all the rights and privileges. There is no sin too great the Father will not forgive, offering redemption, restoration, and life abundant. Come home and be found in him.

Becoming "And So" People

And so John the Baptist appeared …

—Mark 1:2–3 (NIV)

The Old Testament ends by pointing to the one preparing the way for the Messiah. In opening his gospel, Mark trumpets, "A voice of one calling in the wilderness." The forerunner to the Christ surely was an important person, one to celebrate and follow. And yet I find it curious that Mark introduces John the Baptist almost as a side note. The NIV translation includes the words "and so" at the beginning of verse 4. God promised to send the Messiah, but before he would, he would send a messenger ahead of time to herald the coming. This was the headline, not John. It was a forgone conclusion. It was almost as if Mark were asking, "Are you surprised God did what he said?"

"And so, John the Baptist appeared" is not very impressive yet perfect for the one who would prepare the way. It's perfect for the one who said, "He must increase while I must decrease" (John 3:30) and "I should be baptized by you" (Matt. 3:14). John represented what we should strive to become, "and so" people.

What do I mean by that? So often we seek the limelight when doing acts of service. We want titles like deacon, elder, or some other recognition. Whether we consciously admit it or not, we don't want to go unnoticed or unrecognized. We want to be recognized somehow and in some way. When we are recognized, we act embarrassed as if we didn't want the praise, but we feel snubbed if our efforts are not applauded or reciprocated in some manner. Deep down inside all of us, this is true.

John the Baptist gave us a different picture of what it looks like to serve. Mark delivered it beautifully by depicting John's arrival as a side note, "and so." John's purpose was to call the people to repentance, to turn the hearts of the fathers back to their children, and to turn the hearts of the children back to their fathers (Mal. 3:1, 4:5–6). John's mission was to reflect God's passion for his people (Isa. 40:3–5). When the crowds would ask him if he were the one prophesied to come, he would simply point them to the Christ. Everything he was doing pointed to the Messiah. He didn't want praise or adoration. He didn't want attention. He simply wanted to prepare the way for the King. How do you prepare the way for the King? Do you find that you are pointing out the things you are doing or what Christ has done on your behalf?

When pointing others to Christ or doing other acts, scripture tells us two things that we would do well to listen to.

1. Jesus tells us to serve quietly and without notice, "But when you give to the needy, do not let your left hand know what your right hand is doing, so that your giving may be in secret. Then your Father, who sees what is done in secret, will reward you" (Matt. 6:3–4).
2. Jesus gave a picture of the message to share while serving, "Go home to your family and tell them how much the Lord has done for you, and how he has had mercy on you" (Mark 5:19).

When we find our comfort in Jesus, we find our strength and courage.

This point is worthy of emphasizing: great energy, great joy, and great purpose are found in being "and so" people. This was the point Isaiah was making in 40:31, "but they who wait for the LORD shall renew their strength; they shall mount up with wings like eagles; they shall run and not be weary; they shall walk and not faint."

Hear the words of Spurgeon.

> And mind this, before you begin Christ's service, always seek his presence and help. Do not enter upon any work for the Lord without having first seen the face of the King in his beauty; and in the work often recall your mind from what you are doing, to him for whom you are doing it, and by whom you are doing it; and when the work is completed, do not throw up your cap, and say, "Well done, self!" ... When we have done all, we are still unprofitable servants; we have only done that which it was our duty to do. So, if you are as humble as you are active, as lowly as you are energetic, you may keep with Christ, and yet go about his errands to the ends of the earth; and I reckon this to be the happiest experience that any one of us can reach this side of the gates of pearl. The Lord bless you, and bring you there, for Christ's sake! Amen.[1]

Being an "and so" person is a blessing. All of us who call upon his name are "and so" people. Will you be one too? He is not just the "Reason for the Season," as we say at Christmas; he is the "Reason for Being."

The Promise of the Prophecy

> But they who wait for the LORD shall renew their strength; they shall mount up with wings like eagles; they shall run and not be weary; they shall walk and not faint.
>
> —Isaiah 40:31

Have you ever wondered how John the Baptist could have worked tirelessly to point people to the Christ? His work was to turn the hearts of the fathers back to their children and the hearts of the children back to their fathers. Have you ever wondered how the apostle Paul could work tirelessly in turning the whole Roman world on its head for the gospel in so few years? Have you wondered how they did it with so very little margin? I think we find the secret in being an "and so" person, a gospel-focused life whose focus, purpose, and reliance rests in the Redeemer, our Comforter. When we are weak, he is strong. When we rely on our own strength, we tire.

We see from this passage that the first Comforter was the Messiah himself. Now, a comforter comes alongside another in strength. That is what the word means, with (com) strength (forte). This passage doesn't just point to the prophecy but a promise so simple we miss it. It goes like this: those who hope in the Lord find their strength and courage for each day (Isa. 40:28–31).

- Where is your hope?
- Where is your source of strength?
- Who or what is the object of your affection?

- Where do you find rest and inspiration?
- Do you feel like you soar on wings like eagles?
- Do you feel as though you can run and not grow weary?
- When you serve, do you like to be acknowledged for your service?
- Do you feel slighted when acknowledgment doesn't come?

These questions point to our focus in life, our motives. When our focus or motives point inwardly to ourselves, we grow weary, stumble, and fall. It takes great energy and effort to be selfish, self-centered, and desiring of attention. The promise of the prophecy, though, offers a better way. When things are done for his glory alone, we trust upon him for all of life's needs, and we look to him in our weakness for strength, the path beneath our feet will be easy, grace for the journey will be found, and the unknown will be met with all courage. In this promise, we find our chief end in life, to glorify God and enjoy him forever. There is no me within life's aim, only God. In glorifying God, there is no end to enjoyment, contentment, peace, and hope. There is no end to strength and courage because he supplies it.

Will you find the promise of the prophecy today? Will you rest in the arms of the Comforter? "They who wait for the Lord shall renew their strength; they shall mount up with wings like eagles; they shall run and not be weary; they shall walk and not faint" (Isa. 40:31).

Real Life for God's Glory

So whether you eat or drink or whatever you do, do it all for the glory of God.

—1 Corinthians 10:31

When my son was in middle school, I coached his basketball team. At each practice, we took time to look at what this passage meant across all of life and how it applied to basketball. I would ask the boys why they shot free throws. Their response was "to be God's glory, Coach." I would ask them why they ran laps around the court, played defense, dribbled the ball, and passed the ball. Their response was "to be God's glory, Coach." I would then ask them, "If that is why you play, then how should you play?" Their response was to be, "Our very best, Coach."

This might sound like legalism or works-based living. However, that is not what I taught the boys during our devotion time at practice. Rather, how we live flows from the object of our affection. It is not about checklists; it is about relationships. It is about having been loved, accepted, and forgiven and giving the same away. It is about doing everything to his glory because we love him.

In Luke 15:11–32, Jesus tells the story of the prodigal son. Within the story, we see a son come to his father, demand his inheritance, leave for a far-off land, and squander what was graciously given. We then see the son come to his senses, return home in humility, repent of his sins, and submit to the father's sentence. I always found it interesting that the story of the prodigal son ended at the feast welcoming home the son. When I would present this story to the youth group, I would ask them these questions:

- How do you think he lived after that?
- How do you think he treated his father after that?
- How do you think he loved his father after that?
- How do you think he treated others after that?
- How do you think he forgave after that?

I would bet that everything changed. He lived for his father; he lived for others. Having been loved and forgiven greatly, he loved and forgave greatly. Having experienced mercy, he showed mercy.

Think through some questions today as you look at how you can practically apply this to your life.

- How have you been forgiven?
- How much have you been forgiven?
- How have you been loved?
- What is the depth of the mercy you have been shown?
- Do you consistently compare yourself to others when considering your sin, or do you look at your sin only for what it is?

How you answer these questions will determine whether you are an older brother or the prodigal son. It will determine how, when, and where you show mercy. Knowing the depth of your sin before the Sovereign Lord of the universe makes a difference in one's perspective, attitude, and patience.

I would encourage you today to come to grips with the depth of your sin and depravity. Once you have done this, I would encourage you to lean on, depend on, and glory in the one who died and rose again for you. I promise you that when you do this, you will change by his grace. You will live life for him by loving unconditionally, forgiving freely and graciously, and spreading mercy. You will do it for his glory without expectation of recognition. You will live life abundantly.

The Omnipotent King

And he preached, saying, "After me comes he who is mightier than I, the strap of whose sandals I am not worthy to stoop down and untie. I have baptized you with water, but he will baptize you with the Holy Spirit."

—Mark 1:7–8

These verses say, "And he preached, saying …" John the Baptist's message was one of power, position, and promise. It was a sermon for the ages. The omnipotent King would crash through time and space and become a man. The Creator would walk, talk, live, and breathe, bringing salvation and renewal to a creation broken and moaning under the weight of sin. The message offered a breathtaking look at the omnipotent King who loved his people enough to become like them in every respect, save sin, in order to redeem them. It offered the hope of the gospel, "He will baptize you with the Holy Spirit" (Mark 1:8). What a message for the people to hear!

The three-point sermon starts out, "After me comes he who is mightier than I" (Mark 1:7). John starts by pointing to the Messiah's power. Jesus displayed this in every respect: raising people from the dead; healing people of disease; controlling storms; driving out demons; providing food for the hungry; and, if that were not enough, rising from the dead, defeating death and sin. John saw this and marveled at it. As people were looking at him, John was saying, "You need to look at the one who comes after me. He is the one, not me."

He continued, "the strap of whose sandals I am not worthy to stoop down and untie" (Mark 1:7). This act of untying a sandal was to be done by the lowliest servant. When John compares himself to the Messiah, he realizes he is not worthy even to untie them, that he is not even the lowliest of servants. In this second point, John points to the position of the Christ. He was not only more powerful but preeminent and exalted. In his humility, he understood he was not worthy to even be in his presence. Yet, in his humility, he found himself lifted up by the one who is lifted up (Matt. 11:11; Phil 2:9). John understood his sinfulness and God's holiness. We see this in the exchange he had with Christ, expressing the need to be baptized by him (Matt. 3:14). John knew he was a sinner in need of a Savior. John knew he had nothing to offer and everything to gain. There is freedom in knowing this. The message offers hope as we approach God.

Do you have this same view of Christ? Do you feel you are unworthy to stoop down and untie his sandals? This picture is that of the tax collector in Luke 18:13, "But the tax collector, standing far off, would not even lift up his eyes to heaven, but beat his breast, saying, 'God, be merciful to me, a sinner!'"

Finally, the end of the three-point sermon arrives. "I have baptized you with water, but he will baptize you with the Holy Spirit" (Mark 1:8). This was the promise, salvation for the people of God. This salvation is not something we can do but would be a work brought about by the Spirit. Once saved, we would be made to rest in the sovereignty of Christ the King. In this place of rest, we would be able to live free of worry, full of purpose, and without regret.

By understanding who God really is, we approach him differently, with more reverence, love, trust, and repentance. In the midst of the message of power and position, we see promise. Our sin, which kept us from God, will be dealt with, and the Spirit will renew our hearts. When we understand the horror of our sin, the promise of the gospel brings hope and new life, forgiveness and grace, and newness and abundance of life. Knowing that Jesus is sufficient for all our needs really does change everything.

Jesus Is Greater

He is the radiance of the glory of God and the exact imprint of his nature, and he upholds the universe by the word of his power. After making purification for sins, he sat down at the right hand of the Majesty on high.
—Hebrews 1:3

In a world that seems in disarray and suffering injustice, there remains a beacon of hope, Jesus. Why? Jesus is greater than it all. He remains unshakable in the midst of the shaken. Several points within this passage demonstrate that point: power, preeminence, and position. Let's see how that plays itself out and its application to us today.

First is his power. The passage in Hebrews reminds us that through Jesus, all things were created, all things are sustained, and redemption secured. His powerful word, his almighty hand, and his unwavering purpose and plan remain set.

> You, Lord, laid the foundation of the earth in the beginning, and the heavens are the work of your hands; they will perish, but you remain; they will all wear out like a garment, like a robe you will roll them up, like a garment they will be changed. But you are the same, and your years will have no end. (Heb. 1:10–12)

No plan of men can thwart the power of the King of Kings. The outcome is already set, and I can live freely by his grace in light of his victory.

Second is his preeminence. When I understand he is the Creator of the universe, the Sustainer of all things, the Sovereign One over all that exists, and the omnipresent King of Kings, the direction of my life changes. I begin to live it *Coram Deo*, before the face of God. My words speak his praise, glory, and honor. My thoughts place him in the center of all decisions. His word guides my actions. "Your word is a lamp to my feet and a light to my path" (Ps. 119:105). He is more than a preference. He is a conviction. I live my life knowing that my identity is found in him.

Third is his position. Because of who he is and what he did, I find my hope in him. As a brother, I find my identity in him. As my Savior, I find freedom in him. As my friend, I find companionship in him. As my high priest, I find someone who intercedes on my behalf and cares for my predicament. As the one who sat down at the right hand of the Father, I am secure in my position. Because of this, I can say with confidence, "Surely goodness and mercy shall follow me all the days of my life, and I shall dwell in the house of the Lord forever" (Ps. 23:6).

A Son Who Would Be Priest

And a voice came from heaven, "You are my beloved Son; with you I am well pleased."

—Mark 1:9–13

When Jesus came to be baptized by John, he came not needing baptism for himself, for he was without sin. Rather, he came to be baptized in order to identify with his people and for his people to be identified with him. This act of condescension and humility should cause us to rejoice today and every day because we have a high priest who is able to have compassion and concern and understand our weakness only without sin. Jesus was the Son who would be a compassionate high priest and would intercede on our behalf before the Father. Hebrews 2:5–11 reminds us of this.

The implications of this are huge. When life presents challenges that we are not certain how to overcome, we have one who has already overcome. As a result, we can take courage in confronting those challenges. Where do we see this graciously displayed in the story of his baptism by John?

First, God shows compassion for his people. Rather than descending on Christ during the baptism as a flame of fire, which likely would have scared them, the Spirit came as a dove, welcoming us to the gospel of grace. As Isaiah prophesied, a bruised reed he will not break (Isa. 42:3). Thus, the gospel invites us, encourages us, and draws us to the gentle Messiah who overcomes the chains of sin and death on our behalf.

Second, God shows concern for his people. In the Hebrews passage, we read,

> Now in putting everything in subjection to him, he left nothing outside his control. At present, we do not yet see everything in subjection to him. But we see him who for a little while was made lower than the angels, namely Jesus, crowned with glory and honor because of the suffering of death, so that by the grace of God he might taste death for everyone. (Heb. 2:8–9)

In the midst of the sin and brokenness of this world—not what was originally intended—we see redemption, Jesus being sent to make things right again. God demonstrated concern that his people not be left chained in sin and death. The most hopeful and beautiful words of Hebrews 2:5–11 read, "But we do see Jesus." What a beacon of hope in a dark place!

Third, Jesus understands our weakness and intercedes on our behalf as our Comforter. He fasted for forty days. He was tempted in all ways yet did not sin. He understood our weakness so much so that when he left, he sent another Comforter (notice the word *another*), the Holy Spirit, to aid us in our journey home. Both he and the Holy Spirit comfort us. In other words, they come alongside us with and in strength, for that is what the word *comfort* means. We can rejoice greatly today because he reigns supreme and is indeed a high priest who understands and intercedes for us even today.

All of these points are embodied in the conversation Jesus had with John the Baptist related in Matthew 3:13–17. John wanted to prevent Jesus's baptism. Jesus said, "Let it be so now, for thus it is fitting for us to fulfill all righteousness."

Listen to the last of the Hebrews passage we referenced (Heb. 2:5–11), "For it was fitting that he, for whom and by whom all things exist, in bringing many sons to glory, should make the founder of their salvation perfect through suffering. For he who sanctifies and those who are sanctified all have one source. That is why he is not ashamed to call them brothers." The Son who would be high priest is not ashamed to call us brothers. Praise be to God!

The Conquering Hero

And he was in the wilderness forty days, being tempted by Satan.

—Mark 1:13a

In the garden of Eden, we see the serpent tempt Adam and Eve in the following manner. "Did God really say, 'You must not eat from any tree in the garden'?" "You will not certainly die." "For God knows that when you eat from it your eyes will be opened, and you will be like God, knowing good and evil."

At each of these points, Adam and Eve fell. At each of these points, they gave the ground to Satan. Door after door swung wide open as sin ushered into the heart of man. At the heart of each of these points of temptation, we see the root of all temptations we face.

The promise of the gospel is this: where Adam fell and failed, Christ obeyed and succeeded. When we talk about the person and work of Christ, we speak not just of his death, resurrection, and ascension. We also point to the perfect life he led on our behalf. This was necessary for him to be the propitiation for our sin. So why do Matthew, Mark, and Luke all relate this same event, though Mark, in passing form only? After all, this wasn't the only tempting Jesus endured during his time on earth. But this story is relayed to us to encourage us, provide us with an example, and drive us to the foot of the cross where we find our strength.

Christ met Satan in the desert at his weakest and defeated him. After forty days of fasting, Jesus fought for us. His example, replies, and manner serve as a roadmap for us as we face all kinds of trials and temptations. Have we ever been tempted to think, *Jesus does not know what I am going through. They didn't have this or that back then.*

Let us remember the words of Paul in the book of Hebrews 4:14–16.

> Since then we have a great high priest who has passed through the heavens, Jesus, the Son of God, let us hold fast our confession. For we do not have a high priest who is unable to sympathize with our weaknesses, *but one who in every respect has been tempted as we are*, yet without sin. Let us then with confidence draw near to the throne of grace, that we may receive mercy and find grace to help in time of need.

The root of all temptations is a distrust of God, his word, and his position. We see these present in the garden-of-Eden temptation. We see them present here in the wilderness temptation. We see them at the heart of all temptations that men have faced since time began. Temptation has no other aim than to convince us to strive against God.

So what do we learn from this? We learn that our only sure way of victory over temptation is to turn to God and his word. John Calvin put it this way, "The first thing to be observed here is, that Christ uses Scripture as his shield: for this is the true way of fighting, if we wish to make ourselves sure of the victory. With good reason does Paul say, that, 'the sword of the Spirit is the word of God,' and enjoin us to 'take the shield of faith.'"[1]

What happens when we fail to do this? We give in to temptation, as did Adam. The temptation within our hearts entices and lures us away from God. When it bears its fruit and we succumb to it, we find ourselves fallen in the clutches of Satan. John Calvin commented,

> Those who voluntarily throw away that armor, and do not laboriously exercise themselves in the school

of God, deserve to be strangled, at every instant, by Satan, into whose hands they give themselves up unarmed. No other reason can be assigned, why the fury of Satan meets with so little resistance, and why so many are everywhere carried away by him, but that God punishes their carelessness, and their contempt of his word.[2]

So when you find yourself in a place of weakness and temptation, as we all do, cling to Christ and his word. Draw near to him. Resist the devil. Find shelter in his arms. Remember, when you are weak, he is strong. Trust the conquering hero and follow him.

What Then Shall We Live By?

But he answered, "It is written, 'Man shall not live by bread alone, but by every word that comes from the mouth of God.'"

—Matthew 4:4

In the Westminster Shorter Catechism, the first question asks, "What is the chief end of man?" The answer is "Man's chief end is to glorify God, and to enjoy him forever." The second question is a natural extension from that and asks, "What rule hath God given to direct us how we may glorify and enjoy him?" The answer is "The Word of God, which is contained in the Scriptures of the Old and New Testaments, is the only rule to direct us how we may glorify and enjoy him." The third question finishes the series for us by asking, "What do the Scriptures principally teach?" The answer is "The Scriptures principally teach, what man is to believe concerning God, and what duty God requires of man."

These questions don't just get at how we should live but what should we live by. As the psalmist stated, "Your word is a lamp to my feet and a light to my path" (Ps. 119:105) and "Your testimonies are my heritage forever, for they are the joy of my heart" (Ps. 119:111).

When thinking through the temptation in the wilderness and the words of Christ rebuffing Satan, I am humbled and ashamed for my lack of faith, love, and fight for my King. I quickly surrender rather than raise my shield and draw the sword. John Calvin wrote, "Though we are convinced, that all our support, and aid, and comfort, depend on the blessing of God, yet our senses allure and draw us away, to seek assistance from Satan, as if God alone were not enough."[1]

I forget that he is enough for me. I forget that I should crave his word more than food. I forget what he has done for me. I forget my source of strength and life and being. I forget … I forget … I forget … Like the Israelites of old, I have forgotten how he redeemed me and take credit for my good fortune, which is really just part of his common grace.

As we think about the temptation in the wilderness today, consider these passages from the Old Testament. They will surely help remind us again of his great grace, patience, mercy, faithfulness, and forgiveness.

- "Hear, O Israel: The Lord our God, the Lord is one. You shall love the Lord your God with all your heart and with all your soul and with all your might. And these words that I command you today shall be on your heart. You shall teach them diligently to your children, and shall talk of them when you sit in your house, and when you walk by the way, and when you lie down, and when you rise." (Deut. 6:4–7)
- "And he humbled you and let you hunger and fed you with manna, which you did not know, nor did your fathers know, that he might make you know that man does not live by bread alone, but man lives by every word that comes from the mouth of the Lord." (Deut. 8:3)
- "Beware lest you say in your heart, 'My power and the might of my hand have gotten me this wealth.' You shall remember the Lord your God, for it is he who gives you power to get wealth, that he may confirm his covenant that he swore to your fathers, as it is this day." (Deut. 8:17–18)

What then shall we live by? Every word proceeding from his mouth shall be a light to our path. Let us crave it more than food itself. It shall be a remembrance to us of his great love, mercy, faithfulness, and forgiveness. Let us sing of the mercies of the Lord forever. It shall serve as a beacon of hope in a wilderness land filled with scorpions and serpents pointing to the Promised Land of his future kingdom, a place he promised to prepare for us. Let us long for that day when our King returns and makes all things new. We don't have to fall prey to Satan's attacks. We have the example of Christ. Let us rely upon him, raise our shield, and draw our swords.

A Message at Just the Right Time

Now after John was arrested, Jesus came into Galilee, proclaiming the gospel of God, and saying, "The time is fulfilled, and the kingdom of God is at hand; repent and believe in the gospel."

—Mark 1:14–15

We had John the Baptist's sermon in verses 7–8. If you recall, we mentioned earlier that his message was one of power, position, and promise. It was a sermon for the ages. The omnipotent King would crash through time and space and become a man. The Creator would walk, talk, live, and breathe, bringing salvation and renewal to a creation broken and moaning under the weight of sin. The message offered a breathtaking look at the omnipotent King who loved his people enough to become like them in every respect, save sin, in order to redeem them. It offered the hope of the gospel, "he will baptize you with the Holy Spirit" (Mark 1:8).

Now, in verses 14–15, we have the sermon of Christ. It contains three points as well: the time is fulfilled, the kingdom of God is at hand, and repent and believe the gospel. It's very simple and yet full of meaning.

It is interesting when Sunday school teachers come to me and ask, "How should I handle or teach such and such a passage?" I always respond this way, "Run to the gospel." This is what Jesus does in his sermon. It is a lesson we should all listen to. Instead of trying to be clever, simply preach the gospel. Let's walk through these two verses and see what they might say to us today.

The first thing to note in this passage is the words, "Now after John was arrested." The ministry of Christ was timed perfectly by the Father and carried out by the Son in accordance with that plan. As we saw previously, a forerunner came to point people to the fact that the Messiah was coming and indeed was in their midst. As long as that message was being proclaimed, Jesus remained silent. Jesus would not compete with that ministry of preparation but patiently waited until the appointed time to proclaim the good news of the gospel.

Second, the passage shows us God deliberately acting in time and space to redeem his people, "The time is fulfilled." Jesus came at just the right time, not a second too early or a second too late. Romans 5:6 reminds us, "For while we were still weak, *at the right time* Christ died for the ungodly." In Galatians 4:4–5, we read, *"But when the fullness of time had come,* God sent forth his Son, born of woman, born under the law, 5 to redeem those who were under the law, so that we might receive adoption as sons." And again, we read in Ephesians 1:7–10, "In him we have redemption through his blood, the forgiveness of our trespasses, according to the riches of his grace, which he lavished upon us, in all wisdom and insight making known to us the mystery of his will, according to his purpose, which he set forth in Christ *as a plan for the fullness of time,* to unite all things in him, things in heaven and things on earth."

From before the foundations of the world, God planned to rescue you and me from sin and death. Jesus bursts through the scene and declares, "The time has come. It is fulfilled in me." Praise be to God for what he has done on our behalf! Let us rejoice and be glad that our Savior came to live the perfect life that we could not so he could pay the penalty for sin that we deserved in order to rise again, conquering sin and death.

Third, the message was clear, "the kingdom of God is near." I am reminded of how John Calvin in his *Commentaries* declared (I am paraphrasing) that the kingdom of God was nothing less than men and women who were far off being once again brought together under the rule and authority of God through a free adoption of grace and mercy.[1] We are called to return to him, submit to his rule, love him, glorify him, and enjoy him forever. We are called to reconciliation and restoration, peace and hope, and life abundance. The kingdom of God is near to us today, just as it was two thousand years ago. How will you respond?

Fourth, the way of salvation was clear, faith and repentance. Jesus said, "Repent and believe in the gospel." Oh, how we try to complicate the message! Christ made it so simple. Put your faith in Christ. No works are needed, for he took care of it all. It is by grace alone through faith alone.

Fifth, the example for us is clear, one of witness. Just as Christ came to seek and save that which was lost, we are to seek out those who are lost so we can point them to the one who can save, redeem, and restore. He serves as the example of how we should spread the gospel message.

What then should we do with this today? Rejoice in what he has done on our behalf. Rejoice in the message of the kingdom of God. Share with others what God has done for you, how he has blessed you, and how he has been gracious to you. Call people to repent and believe, for the kingdom of God is indeed at hand. Do it with compassion. Do it with boldness. This is indeed a message for all time.

The Call to Return

Have this mind among yourselves, which is yours in Christ Jesus.
—Philippians 2:5

The call to repent was central to both John's and Jesus's message. "Repent, for the Kingdom of God is near!" they shouted. This idea of repentance meant more than just changing directions. It was the picture of the prodigal son in the pigpen in Luke 15. The Greek concept of repentance came from the word *metanoia*. It literally means a thought that came too late, almost like you smacking your forehead, saying, "I can't believe I did that." It also carries with it a change resulting from that sorrowful feeling.

Repentance is about acknowledging sin, being truly sorry, receiving forgiveness, desiring to turn away, and, in humility, relying on the one who frees us from sin. Fleeing is a key component of repentance. There are no excuses, no blame-shifting, and no minimizing the gravity of the sin. The question comes to mind, though, *If we are repenting of our sins and fleeing, where do we flee, and what do we do?*

First, we flee to Christ alone. Whether we are repenting of sin already committed or wrestling with the devil himself, we should, as James wrote, "Submit yourselves therefore to God." When we do this, we will find the strength and courage to "resist the devil," and we will experience comfort, as "he will flee from you" (James 4:7).

James gave us this insight that victory over sin comes not through our strength or programs but by God's strength and comfort.

Second, we imitate Christ alone. Paul said to the church in Philippi,

> So if there is any encouragement in Christ, any comfort from love, any participation in the Spirit, any affection and sympathy, complete my joy by being of the same mind, having the same love, being in full accord and of one mind. Do nothing from selfish ambition or conceit, but in humility count others more significant than yourselves. Let each of you look not only to his own interests, but also to the interests of others. Have this mind among yourselves, which is yours in Christ Jesus. (Phil. 2:1-5)

Notice what you do to imitate Christ in this passage.

- Being like-minded
- Having the same love
- Being one in spirit and of one mind
- Doing nothing out of selfish ambition
- Doing nothing out of vain conceit
- Valuing others above yourselves
- Looking to the interests of others

How are you doing? If you find that you are falling short in any of these areas, ask God for grace to repent and start fresh.

In this letter, Paul reminds us of the source of our actions, God himself. Hear what he says, "So if there is any encouragement in Christ, any comfort from love, any participation in the Spirit, any affection and sympathy, complete my joy." We should receive encouragement from being united with Christ. We should receive great strength from his love. We should experience the community of the saints. We should demonstrate tenderness and be willing to enter into suffering with and for our brothers and sisters. We do this all through Christ. The call to repent is clear. The path before you is sure. Will you take it today?

His Call to Service

Passing alongside the Sea of Galilee, he saw Simon and Andrew the brother of Simon casting a net into the sea, for they were fishermen. And Jesus said to them, "Follow me, and I will make you become fishers of men." And immediately they left their nets and followed him. And going on a little farther, he saw James the son of Zebedee and John his brother, who were in their boat mending the nets. And immediately he called them, and they left their father Zebedee in the boat with the hired servants and followed him.

—Mark 1:16–20

In this passage, Jesus calls his first disciples. Three things stand out to me as I read through this passage: the command, the promise, and the response. All of these are wrapped up in the fact that evangelism is his plan to spread the gospel message. There is no plan B. We see this clearly in Romans 10.

How then will they call on him in whom they have not believed? And how are they to believe in him of whom they have never heard? And how are they to hear without someone preaching? And how are they to preach unless they are sent? As it is written, "How beautiful are the feet of those who preach the good news!" But they have not all obeyed the gospel. For Isaiah says, "Lord, who has believed what he has heard from us?" So faith comes from hearing, and hearing through the word of Christ. (Rom. 10:14–17)

So the first thing to note here is the command, "Follow me." His call clearly requires a heart that has been changed. The message is clear: leave behind the things of the past, give up what is comfortable, and submit to his leadership. It doesn't always mean that we give up our occupation, but it might. This might seem uncomfortable. But within this call is the clear picture that he must be both Lord and Savior. A. W. Tozer said we cannot believe in a half-Christ. He must be both Lord and Savior. We must trust, obey, and follow. This is all of faith.[1]

Second is the promise, "I will make you become fishers of men." He will not only send you; he will prepare and provide all that is necessary for this role. Paul said in Ephesians 2:10, "For we are his workmanship, created in Christ Jesus for good works, which God prepared beforehand, that we should walk in them." And again, in 2 Timothy 3:16–17, we read, "All Scripture is breathed out by God and profitable for teaching, for reproof, for correction, and for training in righteousness, that the man of God may be complete, equipped for every good work." His promise is perfect and irrevocable. He will make us fishers of men.

Third is the response, "And immediately they left their nets and followed him." The picture of obedience we see is both immediate and complete, without complaining.

The calling is for us today. Will you come and follow him? If you do, he will keep his promise and make you into a fisher of men. Go and preach the good news of God's great grace and mercy and tell others all that God has done for you.

The Sabbath, Healing, and Teaching

And they went into Capernaum, and immediately on the Sabbath he
entered the synagogue and was teaching. And they were astonished at
his teaching, for he taught them as one who had authority, and not as the
scribes ... And he healed many who were sick with various diseases, and
cast out many demons. And he would not permit the demons to speak,
because they knew him.

—Mark 1:21–22, 34

We see three principles within this passage that are worth noting:
seeing Jesus as our example, learning about the gospel message, and
understanding what it says about Jesus. With the economy of words
we see in Mark, every word should speak to us. I see three things as
I discover Jesus in this section of the book of Mark.

First, Jesus saw the importance of going to the synagogue on
the sabbath. Over and over again throughout the gospel narratives,
we see Jesus going to church on the Sabbath. He used it as an
opportunity to teach, heal, and minister. The takeaway is that there
is great value to the people of God to meet with Jesus on Sunday
morning. It is good for our soul. It is good for our life. That is why
Paul wrote in Hebrews 10, "And let us consider how to stir up one
another to love and good works, *not neglecting to meet together, as is the
habit of some*, but encouraging one another, and ball the more as you
see the Day drawing near."

The commandments did not go away with the coming of Jesus.
We are still to obey the fourth commandment, "Keep the Sabbath."

But it is not what you might think. Read through Isaiah 58 (especially verses 13–14 but generally the entire chapter) to understand Jesus's motif when it came to the Sabbath. As you read through it, notice the repetition of various phrases and concepts: pour yourself out, from doing your pleasure, not going your own ways, not talking idly, and not seeking your own pleasure. There is great creativity in carrying out this command within the confines of these phrases.

Second, Jesus healed many. This points back to the fulfillment of what John said, "After me will come one more powerful than I." By the sheer force of his voice, he could heal, drive out demons, and control the weather. That second one, though, was new. Nowhere in scripture do we see another driving out demons up to that point. This spoke to his power, position, and purpose. They spoke of who he was, "you are the Holy One of God." They acknowledged his power. "Have you come to destroy us?" They knew his purpose, to destroy the grip that sin has on the people of God.

Let's look at that last statement just a bit further. Driving out demons was a sign that the kingdom of God had come. In Luke, we read the following in 11:20, "But if it is by the finger of God that I cast out demons, then the kingdom of God has come upon you." He was validating the sermon message, "The kingdom of God is at hand." It is as if he is saying, "Salvation has come."

And just like that, before television, radio, newspapers, or the internet, the fame of Christ spread. People started to hear about this person working wonders. *Could it be?* they had to have thought. After all, there had been prophets in Israel throughout the Old Testament period. It was as if under every rock and behind every bush, there was a prophet. Then for four hundred years ... silence. Now, Christ speaks and heals, and the people don't know what is going on.

Finally, his teaching was full of authority and amazed the people. Matthew Henry said, "But Christ taught as one that had authority, as one that knew the mind of God, and was commissioned to declare it. There is much in the doctrine of Christ, that is astonishing; the more we hear it, the more cause we shall see to admire it."[1]

The word of God was in his bones. When he spoke, people

could see it. There was nothing fanciful about it. There was nothing flashy. He was not trying to impress or generate large numbers to show up on Sunday morning. Rather, he preached the gospel, which is a stumbling block to the wise, to those who think they can save themselves.

So what is the application? Do you look with eagerness to Sunday morning worship to meet your Savior? Do you cherish the word of God read and expounded with care? Do you look with great anticipation for the healing of the ails of this life by the one who heals? Or do you go with dread and hope it lasts no longer than an hour? I pray we can take from the example of Jesus the value of these things.

Prayer: Connecting with the Father

And rising very early in the morning, while it was still dark, he departed
and went out to a desolate place, and there he prayed.

—Mark 1:35

Mark doesn't get far in his narrative when we see Jesus going off to a quiet place to pray. In this brief story, we see Jesus modeling prayer for us, not just how to pray or where or when. He shows us the absolute need to spend time alone with the Father. He emphasizes the absolute need to pray and listen apart from the hustle and bustle of daily life. This is an area I really could hear more as I discover Jesus. My prayer life frequently lags. In my selfishness and self-sufficiency, I find excuses not to pray. It seems as though prayer comes only in times of need, hurt, or uncertainty. This should not be!

First, the passage shows us that prayer is a way of connecting with the Father. As I think about this, several things come to mind. Prayer is an indication

- of my love for him. If I love him more than I love anything else, pursue him more than I pursue anything else, treasure him more than I treasure anything else, and know him more than I know anything else, then I will desperately want to spend time with him.
- of my dependence on him. If I truly acknowledge my need for his provision in all things, I will find myself on my knees before the throne of heaven.

- of my journey with him. How can I follow him if I never speak with him?
- of my growth in him. If I don't or won't pray, indeed my faith will eventually shrivel like the seed sown in rocky soil. This story also illustrates the gift we have in prayer.

So what does prayer give us? Prayer gives us

- peace for the unknown. If we believe that Christ is sovereign and not even a sparrow falls to the ground without his knowing, then through prayer we find a peace from worry.
- direction for today. When his disciples were trying to get him to go back, Jesus pointed them to the urgent work in front of them. Prayer gives us clarity as we rest in his sovereignty and submit to his will.
- energy for the task ahead. Prayer reminds us that we do everything for his glory, honor, and praise. That being the case, we find strength in his provision of grace for the tasks ahead.

Prayer is important. Sweet is the time a child spends with a Father who loves him beyond measure. As the hymn writer penned,[1]

> *Take time to be holy, speak oft with thy Lord;*
> *Abide in Him always, and feed on His Word.*
> *Make friends of God's children, help those who are weak,*
> *Forgetting in nothing His blessing to seek.*
>
> *Take time to be holy, the world rushes on;*
> *Spend much time in secret, with Jesus alone.*
> *By looking to Jesus, like Him thou shalt be;*
> *Thy friends in thy conduct His likeness shall see.*
>
> *Take time to be holy, let Him be thy Guide;*
> *And run not before Him, whatever betide.*

In joy or in sorrow, still follow the Lord,
And, looking to Jesus, still trust in His Word.

Take time to be holy, be calm in thy soul,
Each thought and each motive beneath His control.
Thus led by His Spirit to fountains of love,
Thou soon shalt be fitted for service above.

The Lord's Prayer: A Place in the Kingdom

Our Father in heaven.

—Matthew 6:9

During the early part of his ministry, Jesus's disciples came to him and said, "Lord, teach us to pray." In proceeding to teach them how to pray, Jesus gave them a picture of the gospel. In fact, the whole meaning of the Lord's Prayer is a plea to our Father that the gospel would become an ever-present and growing reality in our lives. It is about transformed lives transforming community. As we experience true transformation, our prayers become transformed, demonstrating a heart filled with the gospel, motivated by the gospel, and encouraged by the gospel. Prayer becomes the engine of a transformed life. Spurgeon said, "We shall never see much change for the better in our churches in general till the prayer meeting occupies a higher place in the esteem of Christians."[1]

As we consider the first part of the Lord's Prayer, I want us to see three things: our place in the kingdom, our role in the kingdom, and our obligation in the kingdom. As we move forward through the prayer, we see the central focus and how it remains the same throughout, "hallowed be thy name." Oh Lord, may thy name be hallowed by your people carrying out your Great Commission. May thy name be hallowed as we submit to be ruled by you. May your name be hallowed through our daily bread. May your name be hallowed through forgiveness granted freely and willingly. May your name be hallowed in whatever state we find ourselves. May your name be hallowed.

First, we have a place in the kingdom. We are his children, not hired hands. This is beautifully pictured for us in the parable of the prodigal son. We are part of a family more far-reaching than our minds can comprehend. Jesus said we have brothers, sisters, mothers, and fathers a thousand times over. As someone who has been adopted, I can understand what Peter meant when he said that once we were not a people, but now we are. Paul reminds us that we were once children of wrath but are now children of God. Indeed, we have a place in the kingdom. What makes him our Father? Faith. "For in Christ Jesus you are all sons of God, through faith" (Gal. 3:26).

Don't belittle the point. Christ has redeemed you! I love how George Muller put it, "I have known my Lord for forty-seven years, and there has never been a single day that I have failed to gain an audience with the King."[2] We are his children—valued, loved, cared for, and protected.

- "I entreat Euodia and I entreat Syntyche to agree in the Lord. Yes, I ask you also, true companion, help these women, who have labored side by side with me in the gospel together with Clement and the rest of my fellow workers, *whose names are in the book of life*." (Phil 4:3)
- "The one who conquers will be clothed thus in white garments, and *I will never blot his name out of the book of life*. I will confess his name before my Father and before his angels." (Rev. 3:5)
- "But as it is, they desire a better country, that is, a heavenly one. *Therefore God is not ashamed to be called their God*, for he has prepared for them a city." (Heb. 11:16)

Not only do we have a place in the kingdom, that place is secured.

Jesus said that when we pray, we should say, "Our Father, who art in heaven ..." Why? Thomas Watson, the Puritan preacher, put it this way, *"Dolce nomen patris"* or "Sweet is the name of Father."[3] What he was getting at here is an ever-present reminder that we have access to God and that we can rely on him for our every need. Think about that! We have access to God! The God who created all things, holds all things in his hand, and does not have a single molecule running rogue from his control invites you into his throne room and listens to you.

I love how John Calvin put it, "Let us therefore entertain no doubt, that God is willing to receive us graciously, that he is ready to listen to our prayers,—in a word, that of Himself he is disposed to aid us."[4]

When we say "Our Father," we lean on our relationship with him and his fatherly love toward us. When we say "Who art in heaven," we acknowledge his omnipotent power and providence over our lives and condition. We rest in our place within the kingdom, for that is the place of faith.

Additionally, "Our Father" reminds us that we are one in him. The barriers that our sin builds up—barriers of racism, sexism, and classism—driven by pride and held together by our idols of self come crashing down when we pray in all earnestness, faith, humility, and purpose, "Our Father." How can they stay built if we pray not with empty words but with words filled with faith, hope, and love?

What is the takeaway for this today? Even though you were a child of sin previously, you are now a child of God. As such, you have a place in the kingdom. Rejoice and rest in that place. Know that the Father holds you safely and securely there.

The Lord's Prayer: A Role in the Kingdom

Hallowed be your name.

—Matt. 6:9

We saw previously in the first part of the prayer that we have a place in the kingdom. Moving on, we see the second important point of the prayer: we have a role in the kingdom. Jesus said for us to pray, "Hallowed be thy name." The Westminster Shorter Catechism put it this way, "The chief end of man is *to glorify God and enjoy him forever.*" Paul said to the Corinthians that whether you eat or drink, to the most basic things of life, do it all for the glory of God. Our role in the kingdom is to bring glory to God. It is at the start of the prayer and at its end. It runs as a constant crimson thread through each petition as a reminder that the only way we can honor and glorify him is by grace through faith.

We find within this petition the heart of the Ten Commandments. The first four drive the last six, "You shall have no other Gods before me … You shall not make any graven image … You shall not bow down to that image … You shall not take the name of the Lord in vain … You shall remember and keep the Sabbath."

So what does it mean to hallow his name? What are some of the key phrases within these commands? "Before," "Make and bow down," "Take," and "Remember and keep." Calvin put it this way, "The majesty of God ought to be greatly preferred by us to every other object of solicitude (affection)."[1] Hallowing his name means

48

that in everything we do, everything we say, every place we go, everything we put our hands to, and every thought we have, those things acknowledge him, bring honor to him, and drive us to obey him.

When we pray "Hallowed be thy name," we are asking God to make the commands given on Sinai, the greatest command noted by Jesus to love God with everything we are (heart, soul, mind, and strength). We are asking God to make these an ever-present reality in our lives. We are praying, as did Paul, that we would not be conformed to this world but would be transformed by him. We are praying that the gospel will take solid root in our hearts and minds.

Is this what you pray for? Is this at the heart of every prayer you make? Is this at the heart of every petition you lay before the Father? Is it at the start of every prayer? Is it at the end? Where does bringing God glory rank in your life?

The Lord's Prayer: An Obligation in the Kingdom

Your kingdom come, your will be done, on earth as it is in heaven.
—Matthew 6:10

Previously, we considered our place and our role in the kingdom. As we come to the end of the first part of prayer, we read of our obligation in the kingdom. Jesus taught us to say, "Your kingdom come, your will be done, on earth as it is in heaven." The kingdom was at the heart of Jesus's message during his earthly ministry, "Repent, for the kingdom of God is at hand." If it were at the heart of his message, what was meant by the "kingdom of God"?

Paraphrasing Calvin, he described it this way: the kingdom of God is nothing less than men and women who were once far-off being once again brought under the rule and authority of God through a free adoption by grace through faith (*Calvin's Commentaries*, Vol. 16, pg. 319). It is not just something in the future; it is also here and now. Jesus said, "Repent, for the kingdom of God is at hand."

We have an obligation to pray for the kingdom of God to come (Matt. 9:38), "therefore pray earnestly to the Lord of the harvest to send out laborers into his harvest.'" Why this command? Why the obligation? Just as when we pray "Our Father" the barriers that separate us should come down, when we pray "Thy kingdom come," we pray that God will use us however he sees fit in bringing it about.

In praying this way, we acknowledge that his kingdom is brought about by him and not us, that our ability to participate comes only through faith in him, and that our desire to participate is driven out of love for him and the hallowing of his name. John Calvin, illustrating this point, asked (paraphrasing), "What is more hallowing to his name than men and women who were once far-off once again being brought under the rule and authority of God by a free adoption by grace through faith? What is more hallowing to his name than men and women who were once profaning the name of God now hallowing it with praise and worship?"[1]

And to our obligation, we pray, "Thy will be done." The Westminster Shorter Catechism says this about the prayer, "In the third petition, which is, Thy will be done in earth, as it is in heaven, we pray that God, by his grace, would make us able and willing to know, obey, and submit to his will in all things, as the angels do in heaven." We are praying for a heart's desire for obedience (Ps. 19:14). We are praying for God's blessing through a life of obedience (Ps. 119). We are recognizing that the source of our obedience is God himself (1 Thess. 5:23; Heb. 13:20–21).

What is at the heart of this request? It's simple, "Thy kingdom come." Matthew Henry said, "We pray that God's kingdom being come, we and others may be brought into obedience to all the laws and ordinances of it ... having prayed that he may rule us, we pray that we may in everything be ruled by him."[2]

As we pray this, we ask God to transform our hearts, souls, minds, and strength to wholeheartedly love him as pictured by cheerful and willing obedience. We pray that God will give us a heart and desire to become fishers of men. We pray that God will give us a heart and passion for the lost. When he does this, his name will be hallowed.

At the heart of the gospel is the hallowing of his name. Dear reader, may we in all things be about the business of hallowing his name. It is by his grace that we will be about that business. And so we pray, taking the example of Jesus.

The Lord's Prayer: Provision

Give us this day our daily bread.

—Matthew 6:11

At the beginning of the 1900s, a group of missionaries was known as "one-way missionaries." When they received their assignments, they would purchase a one-way ticket only to their destination. They would pack their belongings not in suitcases or trunks as the average person would, but rather in a box built specifically for them that would one day serve as their coffin. They would then sail away, saying goodbye to their loved ones, knowing they would never return home. A. W. Milne was one of those missionaries. When he got his assignment to minister to a tribe of headhunters in the South Pacific off the coast of Australia, he packed everything up. This people group he was going to had killed every missionary sent up to that point. He was undeterred. After thirty-five years of ministry to this tribe, he passed away. The people of the tribe buried him in a place of honor at the center of the village with the following epitaph, "When he came, there was no light. When he left, there was no darkness."[1]

Not only do we see from the Lord's Prayer that we have a place in the kingdom, but in the second part of the prayer, we see that God is our provision, redemption, and rescue. At the heart of it is hallowing the name of God. This is not a prayer about asking for things but a prayer about the gospel being made alive in our lives through the redemption of our work, our souls, our relationships, and our circumstances.

First, God is our only provision. Jesus taught them to pray, "Give us this day, our daily bread." Now, as a reminder, even though the prayer shifts from God to us and others, the focus remains the same: everything stems from the hallowing of his name. Paul said whether you eat or drink, do it all for the glory of God. Calvin wrote, "When we pray, therefore, we must never turn away our eyes from that object."

Christ reminds us through this petition that he is the source of all we need, that we need to look nowhere else. From that, we must acknowledge the life of generosity that wells up out of this phrase. The words *us* and *our* just scream at us to look to care for the needs of others above and beyond our own.

Jesus reminded us that we will always have the poor. To some, he gives more than they need. To others, he gives less. And to all, the command is to love our brothers and give generously to meet their needs. The apostle John wrote in 1 John 3, "By this we know love, that he laid down his life for us, and we ought to lay down our lives for the brothers. But if anyone has the world's goods and sees his brother in need, yet closes his heart against him, how does God's love abide in him? Little children, let us not love in word or talk but in deed and in truth." This doesn't just mean physical needs but spiritual as well. How can we say we love God if we see others so desperately in need of him and yet we walk away?

What encouragement then do we have today from this prayer? We know that he, our Good Shepherd, will provide all we need. This doesn't mean that we will be healthy, wealthy, and wise. Rather, it means that in light of eternity, all the treasures and storehouses of heaven are ours in Christ Jesus. It means that if our Father has cattle on a thousand hills, he has what we need and knows what we need both when and where. As a result, we can rest and not worry.

The Lord's Prayer: Redemption

And forgive us our debts, as we also have forgiven our debtors.
—Matthew 6:12

"Give us this day our daily bread" should grant us great encouragement even in the common grace of provision, that we are his and he is ours, that he delights in us as his children, and that he will provide all we need. It points us to his redemption and mercy, which points us to the next phrase, "Forgive ..."

God is our only redemption. Jesus continued the prayer with this, "Forgive us our debts as we forgive our debtors." John Calvin wrote, "God will not be ready to hear us, unless we also show ourselves ready to grant forgiveness to those who have offended us ... This condition is added, that no one may presume to approach God and ask forgiveness, who is not pure and free from all resentment."[1]

In other words, we are praying, "Lord, as you have forgiven me, may forgiveness flow from my heart now softened by your grace and mercy." This really is a sweet portion of prayer. In it, we find great confidence in our own forgiveness and security in him. A forgiving heart is a sure sign of a forgiven heart. A life filled with grace toward others is a sure sign of a life filled with grace by Jesus. A patient spirit is a sure sign that God's peace reigns in one's heart.

We see this illustrated in the parable Jesus told, which is recorded in Matthew 18:21–35. We need to remember from this parable that the person who owed an insurmountable debt is us. The ones who owed very little are those who have sinned against us. Do we not see how great our sin is against God and how little others have offended us in comparison? If we have truly experienced his forgiveness, we will extend it quickly to others' insignificant debts. And by the way, anything anyone does to you is insignificant compared to your sin against God. So the call is to forgive. The gospel demands it. We must not repay evil for evil or store up bitterness toward others within us. We must forgive.

There is a sweetness of this petition as it points to the one who has written my name and yours on the nail-scarred hands. We find encouragement, assurance, and boldness in those hands. We find a transformed heart when someone strikes us on the one cheek, we turn the other. There is no revenge, bitterness, or anger but rather a resting in the one who would be our redemption, knowing it is assured, knowing he will complete the work in us, knowing we have been forgiven a great sin and nothing can remove that. Isn't that a glorious thought? Isn't that grace upon grace that we have found a Sabbath rest? And isn't there great urgency to show and share it with others? For if they miss it, if you miss it, that grace upon grace becomes curse upon curse. And the greatest cry of grief will be a whisper compared to what happens to those who don't know that peace, that grace. We see in this petition so clearly our place, our role, and our obligation. Hold on to the great redemption that he offers!

The Lord's Prayer: Rescue

And lead us not into temptation, but deliver us from evil.

—Matthew 6:13

We now come to the end of the prayer. We see so much of the gospel within it. It is almost as if it is building up to this great crescendo here at the end. Here, we see that God is our only rescue and that the hallowing of his name is the place of rest. Jesus taught us to say, "Lead us not into temptation but deliver us from evil." From this, we learn that wherever we find ourselves and in whatever state or condition, rescue comes at the hand of God alone.

James 1:13 reminds us, "Let no one say when he is tempted, 'I am being tempted by God,' for God cannot be tempted with evil, and he himself tempts no one." With that being said, what does the prayer mean when it says, "Lead us not into temptation but deliver us from evil"? It is not referring to temptation welling up from our corruption, although we can definitely find our hope and rescue from him in that. Rather, it points more clearly to God's testing of his people. Take Job, David, or Abraham as an example. So what does the gospel teach us in this prayer at this point? It says that if I should find myself in the place of Job, may I find my deliverance in my Redeemer, as Job did. It teaches me to say with boldness that even though he slays me, I will trust in him. It reminds me through the example of Abraham that God is faithful even in the midst of what seems impossible. It gives me the confidence of David that even though I walk through the valley of the shadow of death, I will fear no evil, for God is with me every step of the way. The mission of Satan is to tear down, bind, frighten, and destroy. The mission of Christ is to build up, calm, and restore, that is, to provide, redeem, rescue, and restore.

What a beautiful picture that removes all worry in life. It is as if Paul wrote these words when thinking about this prayer in 2 Timothy 1:12, "which is why I suffer as I do. But I am not ashamed, for I know whom I have believed, and I am convinced that he is able to guard until that day what has been entrusted to me." God will rescue all that are his and hold them in his hand where no one can snatch them out. Is there not great hope for life in this?

Finally, we come to the benediction. It isn't found in most of the older manuscripts, but Jewish scholars say that a prayer would not have been ended with the last petition but would have been closed with something like this, "for thine is the kingdom and the power and the glory forever. Amen." If you think about it, the benediction is a great bookend to the prayer. Just as the prayer starts with the hallowing of his name, it brings us back to that very place. The prayer reminds us that we have been saved by grace alone through faith alone in Christ alone, according to scripture alone, to the glory of God alone. It reminds us that we are to be about the business of glorifying God in all we do. In all our dealings with others, they should be seen through the lenses of "thine is the kingdom, power, and the glory forever." As we look outward with the gospel, in our work and play, in our giving and keeping, in our forgiving and pardoning, in the good and the bad, "thine is the kingdom and the power and the glory forever." May God's name be hallowed through it all. May we live lives that hallow his name.

Persisting Faith

And when Jesus saw their faith, he said to the paralytic, "Son, your sins are forgiven."

—Mark 2:5

I don't know about you, but I love inspirational stories. Something about redemption in the midst of hopelessness gets me all the time. As we come to the start of Mark 2, we encounter exactly that, a wow moment that should take us to tears. Within the story, you have four people carrying their paralytic friend to the one they know can heal him. They confront obstacle upon obstacle but persevere until they reach their destination. Now as I consider this event, several things come to mind that help me as I discover Jesus and seek to live my life for him.

First, I must persist in faith. Even if the path is blocked, things seem hopeless, or I am unsure of the outcome, persist in faith. Do whatever it takes to get to the Savior. I am reminded of Jesus's words in Matthew 11:12, "From the days of John the Baptist until now the kingdom of heaven has suffered violence, and the violent take it by force."

And again, Paul wrote something similar to the Philippian church in Philippians 2:12–13, "Therefore, my beloved, as you have always obeyed, so now, not only as in my presence but much more in my absence, work out your own salvation with fear and trembling, for it is God who works in you, both to will and to work for his good pleasure." The other side of this is how I persist in faith toward those who are hurting and trying to get to the Savior. Do I clear out the path before them, or do I create obstacles?

Second, I should be more concerned with the root of all illness and trouble than the actual illness or trouble. Sin and its curse remain at the heart of all that afflicts. Therefore, I should first mourn and repent over sin, as that is the primary concern of Christ.

Additionally, I should have the humility and contentment in my persistence to accept the outcome. When Jesus said, "Son, your sins are forgiven," we do not see the paralytic responding, "Really? That's all you have? I would have preferred you make me walk." Instead, we see someone who understands the most important thing and was satisfied with that.

Third, Christ is big enough for anything we face. His grace, as the apostle Paul once said, is sufficient. No matter the situation, Christ is bigger.

May we persist in faith, remaining confident that we will find all we need in Christ. And may the fruit of our faith appear in that we do not weary in that faith.

Following with All Your Heart

And he rose and followed him.

—Mark 2:14b

I find it significant that Mark spends time specifically detailing the calling of Levi or Matthew. I realize that he touches on the calling of Peter, Andrew, James, and John; however, he spends more time on Matthew's calling than on the other four combined. Why might this be noteworthy? Matthew worked as a tax collector, hated by the Jews and tools of the Romans. He probably had means even though he was the lowest of the low in society. The narrative in both Mark and Luke tells us that after being called by Jesus, Matthew held a "great banquet," and "a large crowd" ate there. This is pictured for us here in Mark 2:15. Mark describes the crowd as comprising of "many tax collectors and sinners."

Why is the calling of Matthew so significant? In following Jesus, Matthew gave up everything. In fact, one could argue that Matthew gave up more than the others. Peter, Andrew, James, and John, for example, could have returned to their fishing boats. Matthew, on the other hand, would have given up his job the moment he left to follow Christ. Not only that, he would have had no place in Jewish society because of his past. He was *persona non grata*.

What happened next is telling. As Matthew threw a party for Jesus and invited all his friends (the "sinners" of society), the religious leaders began to criticize Jesus. Unlike Peter in Galatians 2, Jesus didn't back away or disassociate himself from those around him. Rather, he defended Matthew and continued to reach out to the lost and hurting. So why does Mark spend more time on Matthew's calling than the others? What does that mean to me? Several thoughts come to mind as I walk through this story.

First, we must be willing to give up everything for Christ, to know and share him. Jesus doesn't always call us to leave our profession, but he does call us to put aside our sinful ways and acknowledge him in all our ways (Prov. 3:6). Jesus doesn't necessarily call us to give away all our possessions, but he does call us to give out of an abundance of his love and grace. Luke speaks to this more clearly in his gospel (Luke 14:25–35).

Bottom line here is this: who or what is our Lord and Savior? Who or what is our provision? Who or what is our hope for eternity? Who or what do we serve? If it is Christ, then we must have no other gods before him. In the words of Joshua, "As for me and my house, we will serve the Lord" (Josh. 24:15). In the words of Paul, "For me to live is Christ" (Phil. 1:21). In the words of Elijah on Mount Carmel, "How long will you waver between two opinions? If the Lord is God, follow him; but if Baal is God, follow him" (1 Kings 18:21).

Second, a fruit of Christ's calling is an eagerness to share him with others. The first thing Matthew does is throw a great party for Jesus with all his friends. Matthew had found salvation, purpose, hope, and life abundant. He didn't want any of his friends to miss it. Those who have been shown much mercy show great mercy.

Third, Jesus advocates on our behalf when others start to criticize our love for him. As the one who stands at the right hand of God the Father, we have one who defends us and upholds us. What do we have to fear? Stephen had great comfort as he was being stoned as he looked up in the sky and saw Jesus standing (Acts 7:55). Others can harm you, deprive you, take from you, and kill you, but there is only one who stands ready to make all things right for eternity. The things of today are but temporary compared to knowing the King of Kings and Lord of Lords.

Matthew gives us an example of true discipleship. We try to make it so complicated when it is so simple: love Jesus with everything you are and, out of an overflow of that love, love your neighbor. Rest in that grace, live in that grace, and pass out that grace.

Fasting and the Sabbath: What to Do?

The Sabbath was made for man, not man for the Sabbath.

—Mark 2:27b

Whenever I play games with kids (or even adults), we spend a ton of time debating the potential loopholes of the rules in determining how far we can go before we get called out. It is human nature. What is the minimum I have to do to get away with something? How close to the edge can I go without crossing some boundary? I even joke, "If you are not cheating, you are not trying." Why do I bring this up?

Typically, discussions about the Sabbath seem to end up there. What can we do versus what we can't do? Spoiler alert: If you are thinking I am going to provide a list of rules, I am not.

Since I was a kid, I heard debates on this topic. "Can I mow the yard? Can I clean the house? Can I do homework? Can I watch football? Am I only allowed to take a nap or do something relaxing?" In some cases, I heard individuals justify their arguments by saying things like, "It is worship to me to be outside doing yard work … I find it relaxing to do this or that … I don't have time to do it during the week. If the Sabbath were made for me, then I can do what I want." Or, and I like this last one as it fits beautifully with our relativistic culture, "What is relaxing to you is not relaxing to me. So don't tell me what I can or can't do."

The first thing to note is that at the core of these questions and justifications is the existence of a checklist rather than a relationship. The sad thing is that the human race has struggled with this since creation. This idea of resting originated as a creation mandate, not simply the fourth commandment. We struggle with this mandate because of our sin, because of our desire to be "like God."

In Mark 2:23–3:6, the Pharisees attacked Jesus for his use of the Sabbath. The confrontation culminated in Jesus's claim of being the Son of Man and, therefore, Lord of the Sabbath, huge claims indeed. To be Lord of the Sabbath meant you instituted the Sabbath. Did you catch that? Jesus is claiming something only the Creator of the universe could claim. The Pharisees definitely didn't like it and were "looking for a reason to accuse Jesus."

Within this passage, we see three appropriate uses of the Lord's Day.

1. Acts of necessity where Jesus and his disciples were walking along the road on the Sabbath, got hungry, and began to pick some of the grain
2. Acts of worship where we see Jesus going to the synagogue on the Sabbath
3. Acts of mercy where Jesus, when he sees (and eventually heals) a man with a shriveled hand, asks, "Which is lawful on the Sabbath: to do good or to do evil to save life or to kill?"

So what are we to do with this? Thinking back to the beginning and the excuses we frequently give, the glaring motive behind each is a selfish heart. Each of those excuses center around me. The problem with that is this: if we have been called to honor the Lord's Day differently than the other days, we must think about it differently. Nitpicking is the wrong approach. Trying to find loopholes is the wrong approach. Rather, moving to a different way of thinking that puts others first, yourself last, and God always is a better approach.

What might that look like? Isaiah 58:13–14 gives us a picture of it.

> If you turn back your foot from the Sabbath, from doing your pleasure on my holy day, and call the Sabbath a delight and the holy day of the LORD

honorable; if you honor it, not going your own ways, or seeking your own pleasure, or talking idly; then you shall take delight in the LORD, and I will make you ride on the heights of the earth; I will feed you with the heritage of Jacob your father, for the mouth of the LORD has spoken.

Do you notice the repetitive nature in this passage?

- "If you turn back your foot ... from doing your pleasure"
- " ... if you honor it, not going your own ways"
- "not ... seeking your own pleasure, or talking idly"

This is not about a works-based righteousness. It is about embracing grace and loving him. The fruit of that is seen in how you worship him and show mercy. The things of this world will happen (acts of necessity). For the rest, focus on how you can be a blessing to others every day of the year, especially on the Sabbath. Focus on how you can better love God, know God, treasure God, and follow hard after God every day of the year but especially the Sabbath. Honor God in that day. Call it a delight. Find his purpose for you in that day, to glorify him and enjoy him forever.

But what about fasting? Isaiah 58 seems to conflate a life of fasting with a perpetual sabbath. I would encourage you to read the whole of that chapter. You will find the repeated phrases of not going your own way or seeking your own pleasures but rather spending your life for that of another, building up for another, and bearing one another's burdens. It is the picture of how to live out Micah 6:8. That is a true fast that the Lord is looking for from the heart of man.

The thing that comes across loud and clear to me in this passage is the great freedom given for a life of fasting and the Sabbath. There is great freedom and creativity within the bounds of loving God with everything you are and, out of the overflow of that love, others. May you find his grace to live a perpetual Sabbath and to delight in him on his day. May you find a life of fasting to be rewarding in every way.

Inside vs. Out

For whoever does the will of God, he is my brother and sister and mother.
—Mark 3:35

An interesting word picture runs throughout Mark of being either inside or out. For example, we see it in Mark 3:20–35, Mark 4:11, and Mark 5:40. Because this word picture is used so frequently in Mark and thinking about the brevity of words and quick movement of the book, we should probably stop and take a look at it to understand it better.

Looking at this passage, those inside were sitting around him listening. Those outside were seeking to seize him. In Mark 4:11, those inside would understand the parables while those on the outside would not. In Mark 5:40, those outside missed seeing Jairus's daughter raised from the dead. They missed it because they mocked Jesus.

Jesus plainly gives the meaning of this word picture in verse 35. Those who do the will of God are inside; those who do not are outside. We sometimes hear the words *insiders versus outsiders* and think it is bigoted and hateful. It isn't. It is simply telling us who are Christ's and who aren't. There is nothing nefarious here. It is simply about what defines family and even the priority of family.

First, what defines family is "whoever does the will of God." They find their identity in Christ and, as a result, find a new family beyond their earthly one. What is the will of God, though? John 6:40 says, "For this is the will of my Father, that everyone who (1) *looks on the Son* and (2) *believes in him* should have (3) *eternal life*, and I will raise him up on the last day." We have each of the components of true salvific faith in this verse. The will of the Father is to look and believe. The promise of the gospel, eternal life, follows.

So what do we see here? We see it displayed in this passage by those sitting at the feet of Jesus, listening, and believing. We see it pictured as well in Luke 10:38–42.

> Now as they went on their way, Jesus entered a village. And a woman named Martha welcomed him into her house. And she had a sister called Mary, who sat at the Lord's feet and listened to his teaching. But Martha was distracted with much serving. And she went up to him and said, "Lord, do you not care that my sister has left me to serve alone? Tell her then to help me." But the Lord answered her, "Martha, Martha, you are anxious and troubled about many things, but one thing is necessary. Mary has chosen the good portion, which will not be taken away from her."

The Greek word for *necessary* can also be translated as "needful." It points to a gap in one's life that needs to be filled, and sitting at the feet of Jesus is the only way that will be accomplished.

I have one last point before moving on. In Luke 18:28–30, Peter has this exchange with Jesus, "And Peter said, 'See, we have left our homes and followed you.' And he said to them, 'Truly, I say to you, there is no one who has left house or wife or brothers or parents or children, for the sake of the kingdom of God, who will not receive many times more in this time, and in the age to come eternal life.'"

My wife and I experienced this vividly in Brandon, Florida, while attending Westminster Presbyterian Church. My wife's pregnancy had gone terribly wrong with our son. Yes, my wonderful mother-in-law came down, as did my brother-in-law, to watch my two girls. My parents watched them. But my extended family of mothers, sisters, fathers, and brothers stepped in to help. I did not miss a single day of work because of them. Nothing did they ask in return. They gave all. Into eternity, I will be grateful.

The second thing this points to is the priority of family. Jesus's "real" family might have been outside, calling for him. Jesus's priority was to the "gospel" family sitting at his feet. Teaching them, caring for them as a shepherd, and filling the gap in their soul, that "one thing" was necessary and was the "good portion." You can consider this priority in light of Matthew 6:33 and Matthew 16:24–28.

I ask you this question: Are you sitting at the feet of Jesus? Is that your priority? Do you love the family you got when you were adopted into the kingdom of God? How do you value them? How do we forgive them? How do we serve them? I would argue with the church-hopping culture America has developed over the years that we need to work on this as we seek first his kingdom and his righteousness.

Convictions vs. Preferences

Listen! Behold, a sower went out to sow.

—Mark 4:3

Is Christ a conviction or a preference? In our society today, everything seems to be a conviction. We have cheapened the meaning and applied it to just about everything. For example, I firmly believe that the government is guilty of stealing from the people at the level of taxes they levy. Is that a conviction? Would I be willing to go to jail to not pay what I consider to be legal theft? No. I pay my taxes, every last cent. For me, the level of taxation is a preference.

However, ask yourself this: is Jesus a conviction or a preference? Many in the early church faced that question as they had to decide life or death in the Coliseum with the wild animals. We cheapen the definition by calling everything a conviction. What is Christ to you? That is the question of this parable. Is Christ Jesus someone you would die for? Is Christ Jesus someone you would live for? Uncompromising? Unwavering? Undeterred? Or do you find yourself negotiating him away out of fear, inconvenience, or expedience's sake?

In Mark 4, we are presented with several parables, or teachings, of Jesus. The word *parable* literally means to throw alongside. As Jesus is teaching about the parable of the sower, parable of the seed growing, parable of the mustard seed, and parable of the lamp under a basket, he is taking seeds of truth and, like a farmer, throwing them alongside his listeners. For those inside, the seed would take root. For those outside, the seed would be choked up, burned, or snatched away.

With that being said, the parables in Mark 4 get to these questions about why people believe, why people don't believe, why people fall away, how people can have assurance of their salvation, and how we should live. It is no wonder that Jesus, when he started speaking, shouted for the people to listen. "Pay attention!" he said. "Don't miss this!"

That is the first point of these parables, to listen intently to Jesus and what he has to say, to sit at his feet. We see this within the parable itself as we learn how each type of soil (your heart) listens to the seed (gospel message). Do we let others take away the message? Do we compromise the message? Do we throw the message away? Do we heed the message and allow it to transform who we are?

The second point is that Jesus taught them again. In this word great, patience and grace are exhibited toward sinners. However, his patience isn't without end. There will come a day whereby he demands an accounting. On that day, will you be counted as one who produces fruit or withers away?

The third point is this: do we get distracted by the many things around us that seek to pull us away from our King? Jesus pictured this distraction as birds, weeds, and rocks. The apostle John referred to them as "the lust of the flesh, the lust of the eyes, and the pride of life" (1 John 2:16). Martin Luther described them as the world, the flesh, and the devil. They are all one in the same and illustrate ways in which we allow the distractions of life to steal away God's grace.

The fourth point is that Christ offers something better, life that doesn't wither or choke. There is, within each of these parables, a picture of life abundant, life hopeful, and life eternal. There is, within each of these parables, a call to grow tall for the King, shine brilliantly for the King, and live generously for the King.

If faith comes by hearing and hearing by the Word of God, then listen indeed! Don't let another day pass where you sit on the outside, neither hearing nor seeing. Heed the call of the only one who can save. Pray that the Father will open your heart and mind to his call and draw you to Christ Jesus.

The Response of the Heart

Listen! Behold, a sower went out to sow.

—Mark 4:3

Despite its simplicity, the parable of the sower provides great insight into the heart of man. It offers a gospel presented to all and illustrates each person's response. It clearly demonstrates man's inability to save himself from sin. It pictures a Savior who cultivates and transforms the landscape until the work is finished and the harvest is both plentiful and complete. It warns us not to tarry in our rebellion but to submit to the plow of the farmer. In this section, I want to consider the different responses of the heart to the gospel message. My hope is that you will be awakened and allow your heart to be tilled, worked, and transformed.

In verse 4, we read, "As he was scattering the seed, some fell along the path, and the birds came and ate it up." The path represented "roads" that ran alongside the field. These paths would have been hard as concrete and symbolize a heart so hardened that the gospel message does not penetrate. The birds, representing Satan and his servants, come along and steal away the message of truth, never allowing it to take root. The heart chooses to ignore the gospel message. Yet in this choice, the heart finds itself in bondage to the sin that drives the choice. In that bondage is a hardening that only God can soften.

In verse 5, we read, "Some fell on rocky places, where it did not

71

have much soil. It sprang up quickly, because the soil was shallow." Understand that this doesn't picture soil with stray rocks that the farmer would have failed to remove. Rather, it refers to a layer of rock that comes close to the surface, preventing roots from taking hold. The picture here is of a person who hears the gospel but doesn't want to let go of the things of this world. They openly and unashamedly maintain other gods before him. They refuse to give up those other gods. They think they can compartmentalize God. When the heat of life bears down and they must choose between God and some other god, they give up the gospel message.

In verse 7, we read, "Other seed fell among thorns, which grew up and choked the plants, so that they did not bear grain." Again, the farmer would have removed weeds before planting. In this picture, we see those who think it is ok to believe in Christ as Savior but not Lord. A. W. Tozer once said, "You cannot believe on a half Christ." The heart here loves sin and refuses to give it up. At the end of the day, that love for sin chokes any love for Christ that may have existed.

In relation to the last two responses of the heart, we would do well to listen to the words of Thomas Watson, "He is not a sanctified person who is good only in some part, but who is all over sanctified; therefore, in Scripture, grace is called a 'new man,' not a new eye or a new tongue, but a 'new man.' Col 3:30. A good Christian, though he be sanctified but in part, yet in every part."[1] This brings us to the last response of the heart that we see in this parable.

In verse 8, we read, "Still other seed fell on good soil." It isn't that the soil in and of itself was good. Soil cannot make itself good or ready to receive the seed. Rather, it is only through the working of the farmer that it becomes ready. This is an important point. Salvation is a monergistic work of God upon our hearts. This means that because the farmer prepared the soil, it received the gospel rightly. As John Calvin related, "Elsewhere [Augustine] says, 'How came you? By believing. Fear, lest by arrogating to yourself the merit of finding the right way, you perish from the right way. I came, you say, by free choice, came by my own will. Why do you boast? Would you know that even this was given you? Hear Christ exclaiming, 'No man comest unto me, except the Father which has sent me draw him.'"[2]

Another key part of the response, as noted in the parable, is that all good soil produces fruit, with no exceptions. There is great assurance we get as we watch the work of the Spirit in our lives as we grow in the fruit of faith.

If you hear his voice today, surrender to his call and submit to the plow. Though the plow may cause pain as it rips through the hardness, sin, and idols of your heart, it will, at the end of the day, produce the harvest he has called you to produce. Pray for him to open your eyes and unstop your ears. Pray for a contrite heart that repents and turns from unrighteousness and rests solely upon his grace and mercy. Only then will you find life abundant and full.

What Do These Parables Say about How We Should Live?

Listen! Behold, a sower went out to sow.

—Mark 4:3

The four parables related by Jesus here in Mark 4 provide a roadmap for daily life, answering the most basic question of how then we should live. Because we make it ever so complicated and ever so wrong, Jesus, in these few words, spelled it out for us. The question we have to ask is whether we will have eyes to see and ears to hear so we can turn and find forgiveness. Let's walk through these stories and see the pattern for life that Christ lays before us.

First, we are called to produce fruit. We see in the parable of the sower that good soil grows and produces a crop, "some multiplying thirty, some sixty, some a hundred times." We are called to produce the fruit of the Spirit in our lives as we touch those around us. The fruit of the Spirit—"love, joy, peace, forbearance, kindness, goodness, faithfulness, gentleness and self-control" (Gal. 5:22—23)—should exhibit itself as we live our everyday lives. The assurance of salvation we have is from this evidence of faith blooming in our hearts. However, we do not rest or take confidence in our works but on his alone.

Second, we have been called to be a beacon of light in a dark world. We have been called to be in the world but not of the world.

We have been called to reflect God's glory to the world around us. Not our own glory, for in that there is no light. Rather, his word, his gospel, his grace is a lamp unto our feet and a light unto our path. We shine forth the change he has wrought in our lives. When others see that great and mighty grace, they can only stand amazed and ask who it is who brought about the change. As Thomas Watson said, "Grace is most beautiful when its light so shines that others may see it; this adorns religion, and makes proselytes to the faith."[1]

So do you hide your faith? Do you cover up what God is doing in your life? Or do you gladly and eagerly declare how good God is and what God has done? We are called to put it on a stand for everyone to see, not for our own glory but for his, not to point to ourselves but to him.

Third, we have been called to share the gospel with everyone. In the parable of the growing seed, we read, "A man scatters seed on the ground." It is not our responsibility to change people's hearts. It is not our responsibility to convince them of the truth of the gospel. It is not our responsibility to save them. It is not our job to choose who we share the gospel with. Rather, our job is simply to share the gospel. Period. Simple. End of story. As the writer of Romans said, "How beautiful are the feet of those who bring good news!" (Rom. 10:15). Do not get discouraged whether you see growth or not. The harvest will come. Be faithful in the task.

Finally, we have been called to grow in faith and generosity. In the parable of the mustard seed, we see faith that persists, growing and providing for those around us.

What is the encouragement from these seeds of truth that Christ throws our way? I cannot put it better than John Calvin.

> This, therefore, let us never cease to do, that we may daily advance in the way of the Lord; and let us not despair because of the slender measure of success. How little so ever the success may correspond with our wish, our labour is not lost when today is better than yesterday, provided with true singleness of mind

we keep our aim, and aspire to the goal, not speaking flattering things to ourselves, nor indulging our vices, but making it our constant endeavour to become better, until we attain to goodness itself. If during the whole course of our life we seek and follow, we shall at length attain it, when relieved from the infirmity of flesh we are admitted to full fellowship with God.[2]

The Storms of Life

And a great windstorm arose, and the waves were breaking into the boat, so that the boat was already filling.

—Mark 4:37

Immediately following these parables, we see the application of Jesus's teaching on faith. Jesus and his disciples started on their way across the sea to the other side. What happened next? The story describes a great windstorm or furious squall. To understand the seriousness of the storm, consider the reaction of the experienced fishermen. They thought they were going to die. The waves were crashing over the side of the boat, and it started to sink "so that the boat was already filling." Through it all, they worked to save themselves, bailing the boat but to no avail, all of this while Jesus slept.

At their point of despair, they woke Jesus to ask for his help in bailing the boat. They seemed to scold him with the statement, "Teacher, don't you care if we drown?" I don't think they expected a miracle or thought one possible to save them. They simply wanted another set of hands to bail the water out of the boat. I know I would react the same way, desperate to save myself. Despite seeing him perform miracles, this problem, this storm was too big.

This brings us to the first lesson of the story. Is your Christ too small? Do we think the storm we are going through is too big for our God? Do we think we can muster our way through to the other side by our own strength and in our own power? Do we think that God doesn't care about our problems?

What happened next was simply amazing. Jesus awoke from his rest, stood up, and rebuked the wind and waves. He commanded the storm to stop and the waves to calm. And they did! What was the disciples' reaction? Probably the same as what ours would be. They were terrified. "Who is he? Nature even obeys him."

This brings us to the second lesson of the story. Nothing is too big for Christ. Christ does care. Scripture reminds us that a sparrow doesn't even fall to the ground without his knowing. Scripture reminds us that he knows the very number of hairs on our heads. Christ cares about the storm and our struggle in it.

After calming the storm and seas, Jesus turned to the disciples almost to say, "Did you not pay attention to anything I taught you?" He asked them about their faith, "Why are you so afraid? Have you still no faith?"

This gives us insight into the third lesson of the story. Christ is the source of our courage and is accessed through faith. If they had faith in Christ Jesus, they would not have feared the temporal things of life, for those things last only a season. Rather, they would have recognized that the one who was with them reigns sovereignly over all things, that not even one molecule runs rogue out of his control.

This leads us to the final lesson of the story. Christ Jesus reigns sovereign over the storms of life and can be trusted to carry you through to the other side of the lake.

You might say to me, "Daniel, you don't know where I am at, what I am going through, or the pain and suffering of my heart. You just don't understand." Yes, I do. There was a season in life when I lost my job, my father was diagnosed with cancer and would die, and we were told that my son would not survive the pregnancy and then more, one thing after another as if those were not enough. One storm after another. One pain after another. One suffering after another. Through it all, there was comfort in knowing that my God was in control of it all and that he was guiding me through it the whole time. I remember saying in the midst of it all, "God, I don't know what you are doing, but I trust you will take care of my family."

You can have that same hope, assurance, and courage in the face of the biggest storms that life throws at you. Simply believe in the Lord Jesus Christ, and he will save you. He may not remove the storm, but he will carry you through it.

Let Your Light Shine

Go home to your friends and tell them how much the Lord has done for you, and how he has had mercy on you.

—Mark 5:19b

Mark continues to move at a quick pace through the story of Christ. After the storm, we are brought to the other side of the lake, to the region of the Gerasenes. Jesus exited the boat, and a man with an evil spirit came to him. Notice the quickness Jesus puts his feet on dry land and is immediately accosted by a demon-possessed man. Throughout the story, we see Jesus restore the demoniac man, be rejected by the people out of fear, and be proclaimed to the entire region by the restored man. It's truly an amazing story!

So what are some of the things we can take away from this story? First, who we belong to determines what we do and the condition of our souls. In verses 3–5, the mission of Satan is made clear: to tear down, bind, frighten, and destroy. In verse 15, we see Christ's mission: to restore, redeem, and encourage/build up.

Jesus wants to restore; he is eager to do so. In verse 8, Christ eagerly restores the demoniac and does so completely. Immediately, the reaction of the people in the region was fear, and they asked him to leave. Why? I am convinced they didn't know what to do with what they had seen. This type of miracle was not seen anywhere in Old Testament times. All the other miracles Jesus did were done previously. This, however, was different.

"Letting my light shine" stems from a grateful heart over what

God has done for me. After experiencing God's grace and mercy, this man went to the towns in the Decapolis and told everyone about Christ. John Calvin said, "In the person of one man Christ has exhibited to us a proof of his grace, which is extended to all mankind. Though we are not tortured by the devil, yet he holds us as his slaves, till the Son of God delivers us from his tyranny. Naked, torn, and disfigured, we wander about, till he restores us to soundness of mind. It remains that, in magnifying his grace, we testify our gratitude."[1]

The most profound lesson of the story is that you and I were the demoniac. Do we value enough what God has done on our behalf through Christ to tell others about it? Everyone who has been shown mercy is on a mission (Mark 5:20). Follow Jesus's lead and go the distance for the outcast. Acknowledge that following him might mean going from one difficulty or place to another. But remember that Jesus is in control. Notice all the times and the different audiences that beg him.

Satan is at work in our world, seeking to tear down, bind, frighten, and destroy. Christ has come to destroy that work. The effect of that is life-changing. Will you run to Christ as well and beg for mercy?

Touching the Hem of His Garment

Who touched me?

—Mark 5:19

As we enter Mark 5, we are presented with two stories: a woman suffering from a chronic illness and a dying little girl. After being asked to leave the region of the Gerasenes, Jesus crossed over to the other side of the lake. As was typical, wherever Jesus went, crowds followed. I just find this to be amazing. Before CNN, the internet, and the telephone, Jesus's fame spread throughout the whole region. Everyone had heard about this miracle worker, and they wanted to see him.

The story starts out with Jairus, a leader of the local synagogue. Setting aside any fear of reprisals from other religious leaders, he came and begged Jesus to come and heal his daughter. He didn't care what anyone thought. All that mattered was his daughter. He was willing to give up everything if it meant she lived.

While they were heading to the home of Jairus, the crowds were pressing in on Jesus and the disciples. In the midst of it all, Jesus stopped and asked the question, "Who touched my clothes?" To those on the outside, this would seem utterly bizarre. But to Jesus, it was perfectly logical. This brings us to the first point of the story. Jesus is sensitive to the hurt around him and doesn't miss an opportunity to minister to that hurt.

At this point, we are introduced to a woman who suffered greatly at the hands of the medical specialists of the day. She was, I am sure, at the point of utter despair. She was *persona non grata* to those around her because she was considered unclean. Yet in the midst of her despair and pain, she still believed and trusted that God would heal her. So she went after Jesus just to touch the hem of his garment. She didn't want to bother him. She didn't want to interrupt his daily plan. She didn't want the attention. She just wanted to touch his garment because she knew that would be sufficient to heal her.

What she didn't realize was how much Jesus truly cared about her. Jesus stopped. Jesus waited. Jesus met the woman where she was at with grace and compassion. You can see the words of Isaiah 42:3, "A bruised reed he will not break, and a smoldering wick he will not snuff out," pictured here in this interaction. The point here is clear. We cannot be touched by Jesus and expect to go on in silence. Jesus knew she needed more than physical healing. The woman needed emotional and spiritual healing as well. She needed to put it all at his feet.

At times, I want to just touch the hem of Christ's garment and walk away unnoticed. Sometimes I want to experience his grace and peace without sharing it, but that is not part of the deal. Truly experiencing his grace and peace will transform us into people who want to share it and not walk away when he says, "Who touched me?" Jesus wants to take that burden, hurt, and despair and nail it to the cross. There is nothing that this world can do to separate you from the love he has for you.

At the end of this story, we see the final point. Jesus restores our soul. As Charles Spurgeon once said, "But he (Jesus) is here today … to work the same miracles, only not on men's bodies, but on their souls."[1] And again, Spurgeon wrote, "It was a poor, feeble trembling touch that I gave to Christ, but by it from sadness and despair I rose to gladness and hope. I had something to live for and I had the expectation of being able to accomplish it, too, when I had touched him."[2]

In pointing to a restoration of the soul, the story illustrates the point of Psalm 23 when David says that the shepherd restores my soul. The restoration of our soul pictures the many graces he gives each day that point us to the day when the riches immeasurable in him will be seen. No more will we know the pangs of hunger, these broken bodies in constant need of repair, or the loneliness and darkness in our souls that wonder if we are loved. The restoration of our soul points to a mansion he went to prepare for us, a people he is gathering to himself, and a never-ending banquet feast. We see the eternal future he has prepared for us, a future where there are no tears, pain, or sorrow. To restore is to return or to bring back. The ultimate in restoration is back to Eden.

Do not let this day pass without touching the hem of his garment. Leave the pain of the past at the foot of the cross. Find healing in him. Find restoration in the one who makes all things new. Go in peace.

Believing in the Face of the Impossible

Do not fear, only believe.

—Mark 5:36

As we saw in the last chapter, the story of Jairus was interrupted by the chronically ill woman. What I find interesting is that we don't see Jairus protesting Jesus's behavior or chastising the woman for interrupting their journey. I wouldn't blame him if he did. After all, his daughter was dying. I am sure that everything within him was screaming out, "Who cares who touched you! Hurry! My daughter is dying!" This story is a picture of believing in the face of the impossible.

The first thing to note was Jairus's deep, unconditional love for his daughter. Here he was, a synagogue leader, coming to Jesus, the one the religious leaders opposed. Not only did he seek Jesus out (risking everything he had), but he also fell down at his feet, earnestly pleading for Jesus to come and heal her. In doing so, he acknowledged Jesus's power over life and death, sickness, and health. He believed that all Jesus had to do was lay his hands on his little girl so she would be healed. Jairus was determined to do everything he could to save his daughter.

The second thing to note was Jairus's patience in the timing of Christ. When the chronically ill woman interrupted their journey, he patiently waited for Jesus to finish. Somehow, I think he understood and empathized with this woman and knew her need for healing was just as great. So he patiently waited for Christ to continue on the journey. He may have been encouraged himself by this healing, strengthening his faith that Christ could indeed heal his daughter. After all, if someone could be healed by simply touching the hem of his garment without him even knowing it, how much more his daughter! Yes, I think his patience fed his confidence and faith in Jesus.

The third thing to note is his belief in the face of the impossible. Just as Jesus was finishing with the woman, some people from the house of Jairus came and announced his daughter's death. I can only imagine the deep pain. But Jesus comforted him, encouraged him, and wanted to go on with him. Jesus was not giving up on Jairus, and he didn't want Jairus to give up on him. "Don't be afraid; just believe." It's so simple yet so hard. He was telling him to not fear the news of death but to have faith that she would live again. Wow!

When I was a young boy, Stanley Mooneyham visited our church. I remember it as if it were yesterday. One of the things he said, which has stuck with me ever since, was, "Faith is more than wishing and hoping; it is knowing without seeing; and it is acting because you know." That is exactly what Jesus was asking of this father. "Don't be afraid; just believe."

Upon arriving, the professional wailers mocked him when he claimed the girl would live. So he put them out. They would miss out on God's incredible grace and mercy. Then he did the impossible: he brought the girl back to life. More astonishingly, he ordered the parents not to tell anyone what happened. Really?!? Like no one is going to notice and ask? Here is the point: If you believe, you will be let in.

How often do we miss out on the blessing of a lifetime simply because we doubt? Imagine how those professional wailers' lives would have been changed if they had not mocked him, if they had seen him raise this little girl from the dead? Matthew Henry said, "By unbelief and contempt of Christ men stop the current of his favors to them and put a bar in their own door."[1]

In the face of the impossible, believe. Believe not that everything you desire will come to you. Believe not that riches and fame will be yours. Believe that Jesus is enough. Believe that he is bigger, stronger, and sovereign. Believe that he alone can carry you through the valley of the shadow of death and that, as a result, you will have no cause for fear. Why? Because he is with you. Because he comforts you. Because he loves you. This is not about prosperity or health. This is about a relationship with Christ and living in light of that relationship. I encourage you today to believe in the midst of the impossible.

Grace for the Journey

And he marveled because of their unbelief.

—Mark 6:6

As I write this, Easter is approaching. The passage we encounter is of Jesus going home and finding rejection there. However, in the midst of the rejection, we see grace. "He could not do any miracles there, except lay his hands on a few sick people and heal them." Two things come to mind: God doesn't wait or depend on us to reach out to him in demonstrating his grace, and his grace is stronger than my stubbornness and rejection.

Calvin commented on this,

> We must observe, however, what Mark adds, that some sick people, notwithstanding, were cured; for hence we infer, that the goodness of Christ strove with their malice and triumphed over every obstacle. We have experience of the same thing daily with respect to God; for, though he justly and reluctantly restrains his power, because the entrance to us is shut against him, yet we see that he opens up a path for himself where none exists, and ceases not to bestow favors upon us. What an amazing contest, that while we are endeavoring by every possible method to hinder the grace of God from coming to us, it rises victorious, and displays its efficacy in spite of all our exertions![1]

Truly grace for the journey!

As I think about this, my mind considers the compassion of Christ and the fact that he was the first Comforter. Why is this significant? First, the term *compassion* literally means "with {com} suffering {passion}." We are all familiar with the phrase "the passion of the Christ." Someone who shows compassion enters into the suffering of another. Second, the term *comfort* literally means "with {com} forte {strength}." When the composer calls for the music to be played with strength or loudly, he calls for the musician to play it forte. A comforter, then, is one who comes alongside in strength.

Why am I laboring this point? This is the picture of Christmas. This is the picture of Easter. This is the picture of everything in between. Despite our rejection of God, he made a way for our peace. Jesus broke through time and space; entered into the midst of our suffering; came alongside us in strength; and, from his perfect obedience and love, paid the debt that we couldn't pay. He is our champion from the book of Joshua. He is our kinsman redeemer from the book of Ruth. He is the faithful husband from the book of Hosea. He is the one who would crush the serpent's head from the book of Genesis.

Faith and repentance are at the heart of Christ's compassion and comfort. When we realize that God's grace is our only hope, Jesus enters into the midst of our suffering and comes alongside us in strength with forgiveness, healing, and help.

Oh, my soul, turn today from my sin and cling to the one who saves! Rest only in him for the renewing of my soul, mind, and strength. Oh, my soul, repent and believe. Hear the gospel anew today and turn not away from it. Cling to it. Cherish it. Live it.

The Lord Is My Shepherd

When he went ashore he saw a great crowd, and he had compassion on them, because they were like sheep without a shepherd.

—Mark 6:34

The story of the feeding of the four thousand and five thousand present incredible images of the providence and sovereignty of God and his provision, mission, and expectation for us as we face the world in front of us each day. In addition, it reminds us of our sin and his patience toward us. Each of these items on their own should drive us to our knees in deep appreciation and worship, for he is God and we are not. He is holy, and we are not. He is perfect, and we are not.

The first thing to note in these two stories is that Christ illustrates for us Psalm 23 as the Great Shepherd. He looked out at the crowd, had compassion on them (entered into their suffering), and acted on that compassion to help. Because he was their shepherd, they did not want. He provided for them. He made them lie down in green pastures. He led them. He guided them. He taught them. He fed them. He blessed them. At the end of the miracle, the baskets upon baskets of food remaining were a testament to his compassion and grace. All of these actions are discussed in the psalm and a beautiful picture of the Great Shepherd. His rod and staff (his word) were given because he knew that "man does not live on bread alone, but on every word that comes from the mouth of God" (Matt. 4:4). Surely after the teaching and nourishment, the crowds were able to return home again safely.

The second thing to note here is that the miracle itself really points to Jesus as the Christ, the Son of the Living God. Miracles prove nothing less than to confirm God's message. Satan cannot perform miracles; only God can. Satan's lying signs and wonders are exactly that, the workings of the Prince of Darkness, the Prince of Lies who seeks to deceive the world. They are not miracles at all but tricks like a magician seeking to deceive his audience. True miracles confirm the message of the one sent. This miracle itself was designed to lay home the point that Jesus was the Savior, Redeemer, and Great Shepherd of his people.

Charles Spurgeon said,

> Our Lord himself, referring to the miracle in after days, constantly says, "When we fed five thousand with five barley loaves, how many baskets had ye? And when we fed four thousand, how many baskets full did ye take up?" as if the taking up of the baskets full at the end was the clenching of the nail to drive home the blessed argument that Jesus is the Christ, the Son of God who gave his people bread to eat, even as Moses fed the Israelites with manna in the wilderness.[1]

The third thing to note here is the command to the disciples to feed the people. Although the command specifically pointed to physical nourishment, there is no doubt that he was also encouraging them to share the gospel with a hurting world. For they were like sheep without a shepherd. In another place, Jesus told the disciples to pray that the Lord of the harvest would send workers into the fields. And yet, in another, as Jesus reinstated Peter, he commanded him to feed and care for his sheep. And still another, when Jesus told all of us to go throughout the world preaching, teaching, and baptizing, the picture of this in the story is clear. We cannot avoid it.

Charles Spurgeon said,

Your business as a church today, and my business as a member of the Church of Christ, is to feed hungry souls who are perishing for lack of knowledge with the bread of life … Behold, before you, disciples of Christ, this very day, thousands of men, and women, and children, who are hungering for the bread of life. They hunger till they faint. They spend their money for that which is not bread, and their labor for that which satisfies not … Until the kingdoms of the world become the kingdoms of our Lord, and of his Christ, we are the warriors who must carry the victorious arms of the cross to the uttermost parts of the earth.[2]

Notice the point and thrust of this word picture against the feeding of the five thousand and four thousand. People are "perishing for lack of knowledge of the bread of life." Coming out of COVID, society is facing a crisis whereby the loneliness brought about by isolation is crushing our souls. The crowds are looking for something or someone to fill that need, to be the bread of life. Christ alone can fill that need. This is the point of the story; do not miss it. You are his disciple that he sends to feed the sheep.

The final thing to note in this story is our sin and his patience/ forgiveness. In both accounts, the disciples were told to feed the people. In both accounts, they demonstrated a lack of faith in Jesus. They did not do what he asked them to do. They failed to understand that if God gave them the mission, he would provide. They failed to see the boundless provision of Christ. But Jesus, in his great mercy and gentleness, overlooked their lack of faith and showed them.

What does this story tell me? This story gives me great hope as I know my faith is frequently too small. This story gives me great hope as I know that in his great mercy and gentleness, I will find the strength to move in the mission of his kingdom. My hope and prayer are that through this great miracle, I will find swiftness of feet, strength of hands, clarity of words, and gentleness of heart. My hope and prayer are that I will find compassion for people, that my heart will break at the things that break the heart of God, and that I will gladly enter into the suffering of others to help bear their burdens. My hope and prayer are that Christ will so move my heart to serve.

The Heart of Worship

This people honors me with their lips, but their heart is far from me; in vain do they worship me, teaching as doctrines the commandments of men.

—Mark 7:6–7

In this passage, Jesus shows his concern for our hearts and the sin that so entangles us. He indicts the religious leaders of the day, and even the people, for their false worship and empty words. For many today, this same indictment stands. Jesus says, "These people honor me with their lips, but their hearts are far from me. They worship me in vain; their teachings are but rules taught by men."

This passage is simply an offshoot from the parable of the sower. Jesus, when he saves us, demands to be both Savior and Lord, not one or the other, not either-or. In saving us from our sins, he insists on obedience. So much so, in quoting Isaiah, he reminds us that the heart of worship is obedience. At the heart of obedience is relationship. At the heart of relationship is Christ's death and resurrection, reconciling us to the Father through a free adoption of grace and mercy. This relationship is critical to understanding obedience. Our faith is not in our obedience to the law. It is not in our works that we have confidence. Our faith is in Christ and him crucified. That faith produces within us the obedience required for proper worship of God. Jesus tells us in John 14:15, "If you love me, you will keep my commandments."

Also an offshoot of his teaching is his teaching on prayer. Even there, we see the same warning, "Do not pray with empty phrases." Our prayers are empty because we lack faith and do not believe. The prayers are filled with empty phrases because we lack a true relationship with him. Do not confuse this with a childlike or simple prayer. Those are perhaps the most genuine.

A relationship seems to be front and center to this idea of obedience. Our salvation is a monergistic work of God; our sanctification is a synergistic work with God. When we live in constant rebellion with God, we cannot possibly love him. When we have no desire for repentance, we cannot possibly follow him. When we come up with rules and a works-based salvific path to redemption, we cannot possibly find peace. Within these, we find no relationship. Jesus tells us that the greatest command is to love God with everything you are. Living lives of disobedience is nothing more than demonstrating a complete lack of love toward God, and it makes us guilty of nothing less than rebellion before his throne. If we are to have no other gods before him, then the implication is that we must live lives of obedience.

Returning to this passage, if what comes out of a man is what makes him unclean, what hope do we have? The Law condemns us as we have violated it at all points. We have not kept the royal law for even one second. We have not loved our neighbor as ourselves. Our motives betray us. What hope do we have?

Christ is our hope. Christ came to live the perfect life that we could not so he could pay the penalty for sin that we deserved so he could rise again, ensuring our eternal life with him. He did this to provide us with the new life of grace and mercy needed to change and grow more like him. By trusting in Christ, we find obedience, worship, and life abundant.

In putting on the new man, we begin to live outward-facing lives of compassion, love, and reconciliation, reaching out to the Zacchaeus of our day and transforming the culture in which we live. There are no man-made laws or rules in this, just loving God with all we are and mirroring that in how we love those around us.

My wife and I attended a wedding many years ago of someone

from our college group in Charlotte. They understood what this meant and, in my opinion, worship God greatly in how they live. The wife, along with other women, would go to gentlemen's clubs to minister to the women working there. The husband, along with other men, would wait outside, praying for the women's safety and ministering to the bouncers at the front door. They understood what it means to worship God with their heart and to follow Christ where he might lead. They understood that Jesus went to seek and save the lost.

What is God calling you to do today? How can you love him with all you are, and is it reflected in how you love those around you? How can you transform the culture around you with the gospel of Christ? Pray for his guidance and then go. As Paul said in Romans 12:1–2,

> Therefore, I urge you, brothers and sisters, in view of God's mercy, to offer your bodies as a living sacrifice, holy and pleasing to God—this is your true and proper worship. Do not conform to the pattern of this world, but be transformed by the renewing of your mind. Then you will be able to test and approve what God's will is—his good, pleasing and perfect will.

It is in knowing him and following him that you will, as the passage says, "then" know what God's will is. Glorify God in all you do and acknowledge him in all your ways.

The Persistence of Faith

Then Jesus answered her, "O woman, great is your faith!"
—Matthew 15:28

In looking at this passage from Mark 7 and Matthew 15, what first appears to be harshness on the part of Jesus actually demonstrates the need for faith, the persistence of faith, the inclusiveness of faith, and the power of faith. Let me explain.

You can almost sense the tension. Jesus, being faithful to his mission, finds himself in Tyre and Sidon, clearly Gentile regions. Although this was Gentile territory, it was part of the Promised Land inheritance. This region is where God sent Elijah to the widow of Zarephath in 1 Kings 17 both for refuge and the healing of her son. It was truly significant. Jesus had withdrawn to get away from the crowds, probably to rest. Only he knew the appointment that awaited, an appointment with a woman who desperately needed compassion and comfort.

Earlier that day, a woman arose as normal to confront a day filled with struggle. As she went about her day, the rumors started to rumble through the city. A man named Jesus was in the area. He touched the untouchable, loved the unlovable, entered into the suffering of many, and healed those needing to be restored. Yes, she heard about him. She heard about his gospel of peace and reconciliation.

She wondered, *Could he heal my daughter too? Surely this man who could cause the lame to walk by the sheer force of his voice could help my* daughter. *I believe he can. But he is a Jew, and I am a Gentile. Would he even hear my plea?* At that moment, she determined to go after him. She believed that Jesus could save her daughter. This faith drove her to search after Jesus the Christ. It was a gift from God and the driving force beneath her feet. Faith is needed to move us to Christ.

She approached the King of the Universe, begging him for mercy, for relief. "Save my daughter! She is severely oppressed. Help me!" Despite her pleas, no answer came from the King of Kings. I almost think that Jesus was seeing what the disciples would do or say. Had they learned anything from their time with him?

The disciples, perhaps annoyed because she was interrupting their rest, asked Jesus to send her away, with no compassion or love. Finally responding matter-of-factly and without emotion, Jesus told her that his mission from the Father was to the lost sheep of Israel.. Testing her faith, he wanted to see if her faith was firm in its resolve. She responded in complete submission. She worshipped him.

He tested her further. "It is not right to take the children's bread and throw it to the dogs." Wow! This was enough to send even the strongest home. But her faith was reminiscent of the widow as she pursued justice from the judge. In persistent faith, she stood firm. She acknowledged his mission and resolve by simply responding, "Yes, Lord ..." Most of us would have responded with harshness. She responded in submission.

Then with the persistence of faith, she pointed to the common grace that falls to all. She clung to God's grace with every ounce of her being. Her faith gave her that strength. With that, Jesus praised her and surrendered to that great persistence of faith. Even this Gentile woman would find grace in the midst of this mission. Jesus loves great faith, persistent faith, faith that clings to grace, faith that worships with every ounce of being. Such faith brings people from all backgrounds and people groups to the feet of Jesus. For there is no difference between male or female, Jew or Gentile.

Finally, we see the power of faith. "Then Jesus answered her, 'O woman, great is your faith! Be it done for you as you desire.' And her daughter was healed instantly." Without having to go, see, and touch, Jesus granted the desire of her heart. "Be it done for you as you desire," he said.

Oh, how I wish I had such great faith! How I wish I would find faith to move my feet, faith to persist in the face of discouragement, faith to worship rightly and accept the "No" of my Lord but still persist in faith. I can understand the heartache of a sick child. I know what it feels like to be at the end of your rope on your knees, begging God for mercy and healing. My prayer today is to simply believe, worship, plead, and submit as this woman did and learn to say, "Yes, Lord." May you experience God's grace and mercy in this way. Let us all say, "Thy grace is sufficient."

The Priority of Righteousness

Watch out; beware of the leaven of the Pharisees.

—Mark 8:14b

Jesus gives a double warning here in Mark 8. Hearing that should cause us to stop and pay even more attention. He calls us to watch out for the leaven of the Pharisees. It is an extension of his warnings against the Pharisees that we see in chapters 7 and 11. Leaven was a picture of the pride and self-righteousness of the Pharisees that had no place in the kingdom. Leaven was such a vivid picture in the minds of those listening because leaven affects the whole loaf. When you put leaven into the dough, it causes all of it to rise. This is how pride and self-righteousness would infect the whole of a person if left unchecked. So if we are to avoid it, what should our priority be? Jesus gives us a picture of it in Matthew 5.

Jesus, seeing the crowds that had been following him and were now pressing in on him, went up the side of the mountain. He sat down, his disciples came to him, and he proceeded to teach them. He taught them about salvation and godliness in what we know as the Sermon on the Mount.

"Blessed are the poor in spirit," he said. In other words, blessed are those who see, acknowledge, and repent of their sins. Why? Those who rest on Jesus for their salvation will find that "theirs is the kingdom of God."

"Blessed are those who mourn," he said. In other words, blessed are those who see their sin and mourn for having sinned against a holy God. Why? Those who understand the depth of their sin and trust in Christ are comforted. They are comforted that their sins have been redeemed and paid for in full. And they can say with Paul, "even though I am the worst of sinners," "there is now therefore no condemnation for those who are in Christ."

All these blessings and more he lists. The word *blessed* used here in each refrain means exactly what you might think, fortunate or happy. Jonathan Edwards spoke about this often. In fact, the thing he spoke of most was this idea of happiness. The big idea he spoke of often was that if you wanted to be most happy, draw near to the face of God. It is the exact opposite of pride and self-righteousness. It is humility and acknowledgment of one's desperate condition of sin.

In 1 Timothy 4:8, Paul says,

> ... for while bodily training is of some value, godliness is of value in every way, as it holds promise for the present life and also for the life to come. The saying is trustworthy and deserving of full acceptance. For to this end we toil and strive, because we have our hope set on the living God, who is the Savior of all people, especially of those who believe.

What a shocking statement! Think about that. Godliness is of value in every way. That is a pretty bold statement. It is pretty absolute. Paul is saying, "If you want to find value in life, meaning, joy, and purpose *no matter where God puts you*, trust God and seek after him."

In the Sermon on the Mount, Jesus said the same thing, "Blessed are those who hunger and thirst for righteousness." Notice the words *hunger* and *thirst*. The picture in these words is someone who is literally starving or thirsting almost to death and is craving food or drink above all things. Jesus says we are blessed when we hunger and thirst in that way for righteousness. When we begin to see that "man shall not live by bread alone but by every word that proceeds from the mouth of God," then we will find satisfaction. Jesus said to the woman at the well, "Everyone who drinks of this water will be thirsty again, but whoever drinks of the water that I will give him will never be thirsty again. The water that I will give him will become in him a spring of water welling up to eternal life."

Chasing after the things of this world—fame, fortune, and pleasure—will lead to nothing but dissatisfaction. There might be a temporary satisfaction, but it is fleeting. Why? There is never enough money, fame, pleasure, or whatever. The things of this world are nothing more than a hamster wheel, and you are the hamster. You keep spinning the wheel and keep running, but you get nowhere. But chasing after the things of God—loving him, loving others, and helping others—will gain you satisfaction and fulfillment beyond this present life and into the life to come.

Righteousness Provides Value in Every Way

For while bodily training is of some value, godliness is of value in every way, as it holds promise for the present life and also for the life to come.
—1 Timothy 4:8

Continuing our look at the priority of righteousness, in the last devotion, we referenced 1 Timothy 4:8. I want us to spend a little time unpacking that so we can understand why we should place such a high priority on righteousness. With that being said, let's consider together this verse.

To start with, according to 1 Timothy 4, why is there value in every way for godliness? "[I]t holds promise for the present life and also for the life to come." Notice the word *promise*. It implies something that has already been conveyed or given. Remember Jesus's words? "Whoever drinks of the water that I give him will never be thirsty again." There is rest and satisfaction.

For those who would question and doubt, Paul immediately follows up with this, "The saying is trustworthy and deserving of full acceptance." It is trustworthy because it is based on the authority of Christ and should, therefore, be heard and accepted. The word for *deserving* in Greek is the word we get for axiom. It is a self-evident truth accepted on its intrinsic value. However, it is not enough to simply notate it and assent to it. The full thrust of the full acceptance is a living faith that produces the fruit from it.

First, Jesus said that no one comes to the Father except through him. The exclusivity of that statement is sure. The beauty of the trustworthiness of this statement is sure. All those whom the Father gives, he holds. Those he holds, no one can take away. His character assures it. Thus, the saying is trustworthy. But the second is like unto it. Full acceptance starts with faith, and that faith produces the fruit from it.

Earlier in Timothy 1, Paul used the same phraseology, "The saying is trustworthy and deserving of full acceptance, that Christ Jesus came into the world to save sinners, of whom I am the foremost. But I received mercy for this reason, that in me, as the foremost, Jesus Christ might display his perfect patience as an example to those who were to believe in him for eternal life." A true faith is a living faith, as pictured in the parable of the sower that we looked at earlier.

The idea of full acceptance is not one where you pick and choose the when, where, how, and to what extent you will accept the saying. Rather, the force of the acceptance is that of a glad welcoming or receiving. We should receive it, welcoming the sayings as an honored guest. We should hold them in esteem. We should not let them go, for they point us to the one on whom they are based, Jesus the Christ. And in him, we are assured not just in this life but the one to come. We are not assured of success or fame or fortune. Rather, we are assured as to our past, present, and future and secured by the character of the one who promised.

What does the faith produce? The fruit of the Spirit. "For to this end we toil and strive." In verse 15, Paul uses this phrase, "Practice these things, immerse yourself in them." Faith produces good works, which God prepared in advance for you to do. The point here is this: you have been given a work to do. What is that work? Philippians 4 says,

> Finally, brothers, whatever is true, whatever is honorable, whatever is just, whatever is pure, whatever is lovely, whatever is commendable, if there is any excellence, if there is anything worthy of praise, think about these things. What you have learned and

received and heard and seen in me—practice these things, and the God of peace will be with you.

We have that word *practice* again. Notice the thing about guarding your hearts and minds in Christ Jesus. Being in Christ Jesus is the only way to do that. Our ability to be godly rests in him. You cannot be godly apart from him. The peace of God guards our hearts and minds.

What is the work he has set before us? Galatians 5 details it as we ready the fruit of the Spirit. The point of the fruit is to tell you how you are to live out Micah 6:8, "He has told you, O man, what is good; and what does the LORD require of you but to do justice, and to love kindness, and to walk humbly with your God?" There is much creativity, passion, and energy in the fruit of the Spirit. What are you going to risk for God today? How will you seek to do justice? How will you seek to do what is good? How will you seek kindness to others today even when they injure you? How will you walk humbly?

Before you start looking inwardly at this, the driver for it, our ability to carry it out is being in Christ Jesus and working out our salvation. Hear what Paul says in Colossians 1:28–29, "Him we proclaim, warning everyone and teaching everyone with all wisdom, that we may present everyone mature in Christ. For this I toil, struggling with all His energy that He powerfully works within me."

He is the driver and the source. Without him, we toil in vain. If we are to love others as ourselves, then we will work to fix any injustice, lift others up, and meet the needs to those around us and everything else we see needs to be done with all of the passion, effort, and energy we would to address injustices and needs we have.

Things to Seek First

But seek first the kingdom of God and his righteousness, and all these things will be added to you.

—Matthew 6:33

Hopefully, I have made the point that righteousness should be a priority in your life, that you should practice it, seek after it, and value it above all things. But what does priority mean? That is what I want us to consider next in light of the verse in Matthew 6:33.

Jesus said, "But seek first the kingdom of God and his righteousness, and all these things will be added to you." Let's break down what he is saying. The word *seek* carries with it a sense of coveting earnestly or a striving after. It is what Paul describes in his letter to the Philippians 3:12–14. Notice what he says, "I press on," "one thing I do," and "straining forward." The point of this seeking is that it is not a one-time event but a lifelong effort.

The next thing Jesus says is the word *first*. "Seek first," he says. The word for *first* in Greek does not mean in terms of order. In other words, it is not saying, "In my list of things to do today, the first thing I will check off is this." No, the word *first* comes from the word *protos*, which means foremost, above all, and in all. It is a controlling word. It means, "Whatever is on the list, the priority is to become part of it."

The priority is what follows, "Seek first the kingdom of God and his righteousness." Calvin said that the kingdom of God is nothing less than men and women who were once far off once again brought under the rule and authority of God through a free adoption of grace through faith in Christ Jesus.[1] The kingdom of God is both here and now and in the life to come. It is not referring to the one-time event of our salvation. It is a striving for lifelong growth each and every day.

But what does this mean? This was what Martin Luther focused his big idea on. He wondered how he could help others see what was meant here. He came up with it in two words: *Coram Deo*, "before the face of God." You are to live life—every moment of it, every effort of it, every word of it, every thought of it, every breath of it— before the face of God as if he is watching, as if he is walking beside you, as if he is helping you. It is living, doing, saying, and thinking life for him.

Think about the change in our lives if this were our priority. Would we watch the movies we watch? Would we tell the jokes we tell? Would we turn our back on our brothers and sisters in need? Living life *Coram Deo* is loving God and loving others. It is the living out of the fruit of the Spirit. It is taking off our old self and putting on the new.

If you want Jesus to redeem your relationships, your time, and your work, it is simple. Stop thinking of yourself and seek first the kingdom and his righteousness, and all these things will be added to you. Make it your priority today.

Is Your Christ Too Small?

Who do people say that I am?

—Mark 8:27

As Jesus and the disciples were walking through the villages of Caesarea Philippi, Jesus asked them, "Who do people say that I am?" The disciples replied with the names of John the Baptist, Elijah, or another one of the prophets. To which Jesus followed up, "Who do you say that I am?" Peter boldly proclaimed, "You are the Christ." Jesus ends the discussion by saying, "Don't tell anyone." It's a very interesting exchange, and yet there is much to be gleaned here when considering the parallel passages in the other Gospels.

The first thing to note is that people viewed Jesus as too small. They equated him with one of the prophets, John the Baptist, or Elijah. Not that these were not significant individuals or giants in their day. However, in comparison to the Creator, in comparison to the Messiah, they are simply the created. This is often how we look at Christ as well. We view Christ, his authority, his power, and his concern for us the same way. We don't see him for who he really is.

This brings me to the second point. Who do you say he is? How does your life answer the question? When the heat of life hits, how do you respond, and is that response a picture of that answer? Peter says, "You are the Christ, the Son of the Living God." The early church pictured this as a fish, *ichthus*. The word stood as an acrostic for *Jesus Christ God's Son Savior*. Peter, in his confession, views him rightly. Do we see him for who he really is, and do we rest in the person and work of Christ? Do we see it as sufficient?

The third point to note in this story is Jesus's response to Peter. In a parallel passage in another gospel, Jesus tells Peter that his answer came not from himself or others. Rather, it came from God. There is a very real sense in how we view God, our understanding of scripture, our confession of him as Savior and Lord, and our reliance on him is a gracious gift from God. How many of us, when we approach God or his word, truly seek his guidance and grace in understanding that which he would have us hear, see, and know? Or do we rely on our own knowledge, strength, and cunning?

The final point is transformational and can be seen in Isaiah 6. After seeing God, Isaiah is undone. He cried out in verse 5, "Woe is me! For I am lost; for I am a man of unclean lips, and I dwell in the midst of a people of unclean lips; for my eyes have seen the King, the LORD of hosts!" This should be our response when we come before the Lord. After the Lord atones for his sin, we see the next exchange in verse 8, "And I heard the voice of the Lord saying, 'Whom shall I send, and who will go for us?'" Because of who God was, the fact that Isaiah came face-to-face with him, the mercy demonstrated and received, without delay or concern for the things of this world, Isaiah replied in verse 8, "Here I am! Send me."

Coming face-to-face with Christ, seeing him for who he really is, seeking after him with all your heart, knowing him with all your mind, and treasuring him more than your treasure and anything else changes you. You will never be the same; you will be transformed; you will go where he sends. The look of Christ penetrates to the deepest part of the soul. After his resurrection, we see Jesus on the beach with Peter and the others. Jesus told Peter, "You must follow me." From denial to total commitment, Peter was sold out for Jesus because he came face-to-face with the King of the universe.

Who do you say he is? My encouragement for you today is to see him for who he is, God's Son and Savior. Love him for all that you are and rest in him. Trust him with everything you are and have. Go where he would lead. Be at peace in a world that is shaking. Know that he rules over all things, knows all things, and holds all things together. With this knowledge, be transformed as you draw near to him. When you come face-to-face with him, you will never be the same. Grace for the journey.

His Death and Our Response

And he began to teach them that the Son of Man must suffer ...
—Mark 8:31

Three times Jesus prepares his disciples for his death. Three times they don't get it and respond in a similar manner. Three times Jesus teaches them the cost of discipleship.

Each time Jesus prepares his disciples for his death, he shares more details. In doing so, he demonstrates gentleness of spirit as he corrects them of their thinking that the Messiah would be a political and militaristic figure who would throw off the shackles of oppression of the Romans and restore Israel to its glory.

In Mark 8, he tells them that he had to suffer, be rejected, be killed, and rise again. In Mark 9, he tells them that he would be betrayed, killed, and rise again. In Mark 10, he tells them that he would be betrayed, tried, tortured, killed, and rise again. In each case, he shares more details of what was to come.

In each case, the disciples would not hear it. They would remember this teaching afterward, but in the here and now, they simply could not process it. It was contrary to everything they had known. In Mark 8, Peter, representing the twelve, rebuked Jesus. In Mark 9, they were afraid, did not question to understand, and shifted the discussion among themselves to who would be the greatest. In Mark 10, James and John made the request through their mother (Matt. 20:20) to be given the seats of greatest prominence in the kingdom. They gave all the same responses at heart. "How can you say that, Jesus? When you establish your kingdom, you will rule, and we will be by your side. We will be great! Don't take that away from us. We left everything for it."

In each case, Jesus's response would be the same: he that wants to be the greatest must be the least and servant of all. This was an upside-down gospel in a world that only seeks greatness. You want to be first? Then be last. You want to save your life? Then lose it. You want to be lifted up? Humble yourself. This is the beauty of the gospel. This is the thing that makes the foolish wise and the wise fools. It is a stumbling block for some and the cornerstone for others.

Paul describes it this way to the Philippians in chapter 2,

> Have this mind among yourselves, which is yours in Christ Jesus, who, though he was in the form of God, did not count equality with God a thing to be grasped, but emptied himself, by taking the form of a servant, being born in the likeness of men. And being found in human form, he humbled himself by becoming obedient to the point of death, even death on a cross. Therefore God has highly exalted him and bestowed on him the name that is above every name, so that at the name of Jesus every knee should bow, in heaven and on earth and under the earth, and every tongue confess that Jesus Christ is Lord, to the glory of God the Father.

One day, every knee will bow and acknowledge Christ. Every knee will bow either now in humble obedience or by force in judgment later. Either way, the knee will bow. Will you bow it now today? It is a simple acknowledgment of faith, a trusting in his atoning death, a turning from sin, and following him. Christ swings wide the door and bids you come.

What Do You Love?

Do not love the world or anything in the world. If anyone loves the world, the love of the Father is not in him. For everything in the world—the cravings of sinful man, the lust of his eyes, and the boasting of what he has and does—comes not from the Father but from the world. The world and its desires pass away, but the man who does the will of God lives forever.

—1 John 2:15–17

In his epistle to the early church, John warns against letting the three temptations of Satan take root in your heart: the lust of the flesh, the lust of the eyes, and the pride of life. These are the three areas where Satan tempted Adam and Christ. They are the same he uses today. Throughout Mark 9–11, we see these played out in everyday life.

First, we see the disciples on the road to Capernaum arguing about who was the greatest (Mark 9:34). We see them trying to get Jesus to stop a man from performing miracles in Jesus's name because he was not one of them (Mark 9:38). We see the disciples shun the children away as unimportant (Mark 10:13). We see James and John seeking to have the two places of importance at Jesus's side in the coming kingdom (Mark 10:35). In each instance, we see the disciples concerned more about position than people, more concerned about power than the kingdom of God. The pride of life turns our focus away from the King of Kings and seeks to put ourselves on his throne, even if unintentional.

Second, we see the rich young ruler turn away sad because Jesus told him to sell all he had (Mark 10:17). We see Jesus clearing the temple of merchants (Mark 11:12). In each of these instances, we see the lust of the flesh seeking to choke out the presence of the kingdom.

Third, we see the questions on divorce (Mark 10:1) and the demand for a sign (Mark 8:11). The lust of the eyes draws us away to seek another.

Jesus warned so clearly in the parable of the sower what could happen if the individual allows these sins to take root. If the kingdom of God and his righteousness are to be our priority, then what must we do to fight off these sins?

First, our hope is in Jesus who conquered sin and death. Through the person and work of Christ, we find an immeasurable storehouse of grace and help. James reminds us, "If any of you lacks wisdom, he should ask God, who gives generously to all without finding fault, and it will be given to him" (James 1:5).

Second, we put on the armor of God (Eph. 6:10–18). In particular, we wield the sword of the Spirit, which is the word of God. We follow the example of Christ, who met each of Satan's temptations with "Thus says the Lord."

Third, we submit to God and draw near to him (James 4:7–10). We follow the example of Christ (Phil. 2). We set God as the affection of our hearts and the object of our faith (Mark 12:30).

My hope is that you have found encouragement through these passages. My prayer is that you will find grace for the journey in them.

Be Distinctive ... In Your Relationships

But in your hearts honor Christ the Lord as holy, always being prepared to make a defense to anyone who asks you for a reason for the hope that is in you; yet do it with gentleness and respect, having a good conscience, so that, when you are slandered, those who revile your good behavior in Christ may be put to shame.

—1 Peter 3:15–16

Throughout the book of 1 Peter, the author paints for us a grace-filled, gospel-filled picture of how a Christian can and should live in freedom. Each time, the book points us back to Christ as the source and strength of our sanctification and freedom. As that picture is painted, we see this seesawing between doctrine and duty. Even in this section of 1 Peter, in the midst of his instruction of how we are to relate to each other, we are reminded that our ability to live as Christ called us to live is not something done by one's own strength or power. Rather, it finds its source; it finds its root in Christ as Lord.

Peter brings his readers back to this point in this phrase, "But in your hearts honor Christ as Lord." We are shown, within these verses, that any righteous behavior, any good behavior we have, is not just in Christ but because of Christ.

In Galatians 5:1, Paul reminds us, "For freedom Christ has set us free (doctrine of grace); stand firm therefore, and do not submit again to a yoke of slavery (application of that doctrine)." We see within this verse that Christ has set us free from the bondage of sin, condemnation, and worry. We see that because of grace, because of what he did for us, we can now live freely for him. We find rest in what he has done; we stand in what he has done; we find strength in what he has done. When we find ourselves resting in him, then we truly advance for the kingdom.

If freedom is found in him and I give myself wholeheartedly to him, life looks different. There are no retreats, only faith expressing itself through love, only a life characterized by the fruit of the Spirit, only him and his glory. For that is the life to which we have been called. As 1 Peter 2:21 says, "For to this you have been called, because Christ also suffered for you, leaving you an example ..." Now catch this, "so that you might follow in his steps."

Scripture is full of examples of living for his glory, of following in his steps. For example, Job sat in the midst of ruins, having lost everything yet trusting in God. Joseph refused the advances of Potiphar's wife. Rahab hid the Israelite spies from those in Jericho. Hannah prayed and waited patiently for a son. Ruth stood faithfully by Naomi's side. Daniel went to pray, knowing it would lead to the lion's den. Shadrach, Meshach, and Abednego refused to bend their knee to the idolatry of their day. Elijah stood alone on Mount Carmel against the prophets of Baal.

We, too, can live for his glory as those who have gone before us. We, too, can live for his glory with the same confidence, the same courage, and the same boldness as those who have gone before us. The secret is this: look to Jesus. This is the point of 1 Peter.

For those who think that Jesus can be Savior and not Lord, Peter puts that to bed when he writes, "But in your hearts revere Christ as Lord" (1 Pet. 3:15). Duty always follows doctrine. Lest you think that the freedom he has called us to is a license to sin or a license to live as we please or as we did before we came to faith, Paul also puts that to bed in Galatians 5 when he says, "For you were called to freedom ... Only do not use your freedom as an opportunity for the flesh, but "Now catch this" and "through love serve one another." Jesus calls us to take up our cross and follow him. We are to not take up a burden but our cross. We are to not make sacrifices but to be the sacrifice.

We are to follow him. And where did he go? To Calvary. Bonhoeffer said, "When Christ calls a man, He bids him come and die."[1]

Spurgeon said,

> Learn hence, then, all of you who would have Christ as your Savior, that you must be willing to serve Him. We are not saved by service, but we are saved to service. When we are once saved, thenceforward we live in the service of our Lord. If we refuse to be His servants, we are not saved, for we still remain evidently the servants of self, and the servants of Satan. Holiness is another name for salvation; to be delivered from the power of self-will, and the domination of evil lusts, and the tyranny of Satan, -this is salvation. Those who would be saved must know that they will have to serve Christ, and those who are saved rejoice that they are serving Him, and that thus they are giving evidence of a change of heart and renewal of mind.[2]

When Christ calls a person, the life he calls him to is one that is distinctive. Not only should our lives be distinctive, but they should be so distinctive that people would ask us about the hope within us. Our lives, our speech, our actions, our countenance, our generosity, our love, our commitment, our word, our integrity, our compassion, our gentleness, our self-control, our patience, our whatever should be so different that it causes people to stop and ask why.

Peter calls us to be distinct. He calls us to express our faith through love. What does that look like in real life? It's a million different ways: serving a meal for the hurting, visiting the lonely, mentoring those younger, or spending time in his word as family. In 1 Peter 3, Peter breaks down this distinctiveness into three areas: our relationships, our work, and our worship.

First, Peter challenges us to be distinctive in our relationships. Look back with me at this passage starting in verse 8. Peter says,

"Finally, all of you, be like-minded, be sympathetic, love one another, be compassionate and humble. Do not repay evil with evil or insult with insult. On the contrary, repay evil with blessing, because to this you were called so that you may inherit a blessing." Verse 8 deals with our relationship to those inside the church. Verse 9 deals with those outside the church. In other words, it covers our relationships with everyone.

For example, let's look at a relationship within the home. I will focus on husbands in this example, but it can be applied equally to wives and children. Scripture calls husbands to love their wives as Christ loved the church and gave himself up for her. A husband is called to build her up, cherish her, adore her, and lay down his life for her. A husband is not to make sacrifices for his wife, but he is to be the sacrifice. Whether she loves him back or not, respects him or not, or remains faithful to him or not, the husband is to love her as Christ loved the church and gave himself up for her. "[B]ut God shows his love for us in that while we were still sinners, Christ died for us." Even in our lack of faithfulness, Christ remains faithful and loves us. A husband's love for his wife is not dependent on what she does. When husbands live this way with their wives, people will begin to ask about the hope that is in you.

It is difficult to live distinctive lives if we aren't doing it first at home. As we begin to let the power of Christ work through us and transform our relationships, it will begin to manifest itself outwardly to those outside the home.

We are to love those in the church. Do not consider it a burden. Consider it an honor. John puts it this way in his first epistle, "By this we know love, that he (Christ) laid down his life for us, and we ought to lay down our lives for the brothers. But if anyone has the world's goods and sees his brother in need, yet closes his heart against him, how does God's love abide in him? Little children, let us not love in word or talk but in deed and in truth." The implications of this are never-ending.

We are to love our neighbors. Peter says, "Do not repay evil with evil or insult with insult. On the contrary, repay evil with blessing, because to this you were called so that you may inherit a blessing." Jesus says, "Bless those who persecute you" and "Love your neighbor." We have been called to live distinctive lives in order to draw people to want what we have in Christ.

Be Distinctive ... In Your Work

> But in your hearts honor Christ the Lord as holy, always being prepared to make a defense to anyone who asks you for a reason for the hope that is in you; yet do it with gentleness and respect, having a good conscience, so that, when you are slandered, those who revile your good behavior in Christ may be put to shame.
>
> —1 Peter 3:15–16

Continuing this thought of being distinctive and thus revering Christ in our hearts, we are to live lives of distinction in our work. Considering we spend most of our time during our adult lives working, we should pay special attention to how we honor Christ in the workplace and the relationships there.

Peter says in 1 Peter 3:11, "They must turn from evil and do good; they must seek peace and pursue it." Within these words, his hearers must have turned their ears back to the prophet Jeremiah said in chapter 29,

> Thus says the Lord of hosts, the God of Israel, to all the exiles whom I have sent into exile from Jerusalem to Babylon: Build houses and live in them; plant gardens and eat their produce. Take wives and have sons and daughters; take wives for your sons, and give your daughters in marriage, that they may bear sons and daughters; multiply there, and do not decrease. But seek the welfare of the city where I have sent you

into exile, and pray to the Lord on its behalf, for in
its welfare you will find your welfare.

You can almost imagine the horror of the Jews when they heard
these words. They were to be aliens in a foreign land. They were to
settle there and pray to the Lord for the peace and prosperity of the
land he sent them to. We, too, should pray for our land. We should
pray for its peace and prosperity. We should seek its welfare. We
should work hard for the glory of our God.

Paul wrote to the Ephesians,

> Bondservants, obey your earthly masters with fear
> and trembling, with a sincere heart, as you would
> Christ, not by the way of eye-service, as people-
> pleasers, but as bondservants of Christ, doing the
> will of God from the heart, rendering service with
> a good will as to the Lord and not to man, knowing
> that whatever good anyone does, this he will receive
> back from the Lord, whether he is a bondservant
> or is free. Masters, do the same to them, and stop
> your threatening, knowing that he who is both their
> Master and yours is in heaven, and that there is no
> partiality with him.

And again, Paul wrote to the Corinthians, "So, whether you eat
or drink, or whatever you do, do all to the glory of God." Whether
you eat or drink, to the most basic things of life, do it to God's glory.

So what is the application of this? First, do all your work as unto
the Lord. Do not complain or view it with dread because work was
given as a gift. Do not complain for Monday and rejoice for Friday.
Rejoice in the work he has given you, and do it with all your might.
This posture, this attitude toward what we have been given to do,
will be so distinctive that people will wonder what the hope is that
lies within us. Through my work, I must see others, and I must see
work as an opportunity to bless them.

Second, in your work, seek to do good. Seek the peace and prosperity of the city. One of the main points that Tim Keller makes throughout his book, *Gospel in Life*, is that we are not to use the city we are in but rather to serve it.[1] You can morph this point any number of ways, and it will still be valid. It would still be the fulfillment of Jeremiah 29. For example, do not use your job; serve through your job. Do not use your school; serve those in your school. Do not use your church; serve your church. Do it for his glory.

Remember, God created work before the fall, and it was good. It was a gift given to us to tend his creation. We fell and caused work to be corrupted. But hear the good news. In his life, death, resurrection, and intercession on our behalf, he can redeem your work.

When you find it a struggle to get out of bed, remember Christ. Rest in his glory and work already done. Rest in his faithfulness for the work yet to be done. Dedicate each day to his glory and the building up of his kingdom no matter the work, the vocation, or the recognition.

Be Distinctive ... In Your Worship

But in your hearts honor Christ the Lord as holy, always being prepared to make a defense to anyone who asks you for a reason for the hope that is in you; yet do it with gentleness and respect, having a good conscience, so that, when you are slandered, those who revile your good behavior in Christ may be put to shame.

—1 Peter 3:15–16

I would not want to finish this thought of being distinctive without looking at worship. We are to honor one day each week. It should be distinct in how we live and should serve as a sign the rest of the week that we are to live life in a continual state of not just rest but worship. This should invade everything from our relationships to our work. God told us in the garden and repeated it at Sinai with the Ten Commandments that we are to honor the Sabbath and keep it holy. This alone should cause us to say rather clearly that we should be distinct in our worship.

Peter said in verse 15 above, "But in your hearts honor (or revere) Christ as Lord." Although our lives should be lives of worship and praise, what we do on Sunday morning should be a mirror of how we live each day. Sunday morning worship should not just be a ho-hum experience. It is not something we relegate to two hours on one day of the week. The songs we sing should well up from our soul whether we can sing or not. God's word is something we should feast on and not simply sit and listen to for an hour. This is solely a function of you. Do not blame the church for this if you do not feel like you are getting fed.

How does this make us distinctive? Will people really see it and ask us about the hope we have in Christ? In Acts, Paul praises the Bereans above others for their devotion to God and his word. People will notice your posture in worship. After all, we are talking about the Bereans two thousand years later.

In Thessalonians 5:23–24, Paul writes, "Now may the God of peace himself sanctify you completely, and may your whole spirit and soul and body be kept blameless at the coming of our Lord Jesus Christ. He who calls you is faithful; he will surely do it." To be distinctive means to rest in what he is doing in you. Praise him for what he has done and will do because he is faithful. He is faithful and can transform and redeem your relationships, your work, and your worship. Let us remember that the problems we face are not education problems, economic problems, or political problems. The problems we face are heart problems. People need the Lord. People need Jesus. Let us live lives worthy of our calling and be ready to give people a reason for the hope we hold dear in our hearts.

Spurgeon wrote,

> Let us so act in our work, that there is never the smudge of a dirty thumb across the page, and nothing of pride, or self-seeking, or hot-headedness, but that all is done humbly, dependently, hopefully, and always in a holy and gracious spirit, so that we may expect the Holy Spirit to own and bless it. That will, of course, involve that everything must be done prayerfully, for our Heavenly Father gives the Holy Spirit to them that ask Him; and we must ask for this greatest of blessings, that God the Holy Spirit may work with our work.[1]

It Is Better ...

It is better for you to enter life ...

—Mark 9:44b

Sin is a serious thing. That may seem like an obvious statement. Many though do not see all sin as bad. We have our respectable sins of discontent or forgetting to say "thank you." Those aren't so bad. As long as we are not like that tax collector, we are fine (Luke 18:9–14). As long as we are not like the prostitute, the murderer, or the bank robber, we are fine. Before we pat ourselves on the back, our respectable sins are actually worse. Jerry Bridges wrote in the *Practice of Godliness* that discontent is actually one of the most demonic sins and that a thankless heart toward God is actually at the heart of the moral decay of a people (Rom. 1).[1]

We think our sin is not bad, but it is. Jesus repeatedly reminds us of something in Mark 9:42–50 for when we are tempted to sin. He says, "It is better ..." We might think that sin is better, and we might even feel good when we do sin, but Jesus reminds us that it is always better not to sin. It is better because eternity is at stake. He might be using hyperbole when he says to "pluck out your eye" or "cut off your hand," but he is reminding us that heaven is worth it.

Living a life of sin simply brings curse upon curse. You lose your saltiness. You lose your peace. You lose your life into eternity. Not only do you find yourself in hell, but that hell is an eternity of torment and suffering. It is curse upon curse.

Jesus calls you to something better. He calls you to distinctive living. He calls you to righteousness. He calls you to have an impact for the kingdom of God. Why? Because it is better. It is a better life. It is a more peaceful life. It is a life that brings hope for eternity. Believe in him today, for life with him is better.

Resting in Marriage

But from the beginning of creation, "God made them male and female."
"Therefore a man shall leave his father and mother and hold fast to his
wife, and the two shall become one flesh." So they are no longer two but
one flesh. What therefore God has joined together, let not man separate.
—Mark 10:6–9

"The LORD grant that you may find rest, each of you in the house of her
husband!" … Then Naomi her mother-in-law said to her, "My daughter,
should I not seek rest for you, that it may be well with you?"
—Ruth 1:9, 3:1

In the middle of yet another test from the Pharisees, Jesus addresses
the issue of marriage and divorce. Just as today, there were two
schools of thought around the topic: liberal and conservative. Some
felt that divorce for any cause was acceptable; others felt that divorce
could only happen for a cause of infidelity.

Turning to scripture, Jesus answered that Moses "permitted a
man to write a certificate of divorce … *because your hearts were hard*."
In answering, Jesus permitted divorce but for only very heinous sins
within the context of the relationship, infidelity (Matt. 19). Even in
the midst of this reason, Jesus seems to be calling for reconciliation
as a better choice. After all, this is the grace God demonstrates to us
in our spiritual adultery and pictures for us in the book of Hosea.

There is another aspect to marriage that this passage points to that we seldom consider, resting in marriage. Just as we find rest in our relationship with God, scripture points to a state of rest within marriage. We see this unique picture in the book of Ruth. Naomi, encouraging Ruth to return home, offered a prayer that the Lord would grant she finds rest in the home of another husband. And, again, in chapter 3, Naomi expressed her responsibility to find in Israel a home or rest for Ruth.

Matthew Henry put it this way, "The married state should be a rest, as much as anything upon earth can be so, as it ought to fix affections and form a connection for life. Therefore, it should be engaged in with great seriousness, with earnest prayers for direction, for the blessing of God, and with regard to his precepts."[1] From Matthew Henry's comment, several principles should be observed.

First, prior to marriage, we find our attention varies from person to person never finding rest, as the one is still at large. Once you find the one, your attention, your affection, and your very self should find rest there, from the man to the woman and from the woman to the man.

Second, the connection we find, the rest we find, is one to last a lifetime. It is more than a connection, though. It is a sense in which we are "one flesh" and completed by the other person. Therefore, we should nurture that which completes us.

Third, we should center the relationship on God and his word. The glue of marriage can be found in none other than the Creator and sustainer of marriage. The principles of grace, mercy, and love should find their peak within the relationship of marriage. All of these being true, one can clearly see how marriage should be viewed and experienced as rest.

For those who are married or will be married, my prayer for you is that God will grant you his peace and rest in the midst of the marriage he established, that God will grant you rest in his presence, and that God will give you a passion to build up the institution of marriage. Grace for the journey.

With All Your Heart

And you shall love the Lord your God with all your heart and with all your
soul and with all your mind and with all your strength.
                                                      —Mark 12:30

One day, a teacher of the Law approached Jesus and asked him
what the greatest command was. Jesus replied, "Love the Lord your
God with all your heart and with all your soul and with all your
mind and with all your strength." However, Jesus didn't stop at one
command. He gave a second command that follows the first, "Love
your neighbor as yourself." Wrapped up in Christ's answer is the key
to how we are to live and what we are to do, a holistic approach to
life covering the vertical (redeemed relationship with God) and the
horizontal (redeemed relationship with others).

When Christ says he brings life abundant, all dimensions of life
are redeemed. Nothing is left untouched. We are to love God more
than we love anything else. We are to seek after God more than
we seek after anything else. We are to treasure God more than we
treasure anything else. We are to know God more than we know
anything else. We are to seek after God more than we seek after
anything else. Because God is the object of all our love and affection,
we love our neighbor out of an overflow of that love with his grace
and mercy. In fact, how we love God determines how we love our
neighbor. How we seek after God determines how we seek after
our neighbor. How we treasure God determines how we treasure
our neighbor. How we know God determines how we know our

neighbor. This is the summation of the teaching we see by Jesus in Mark 9–11.

First, we see with the rich, young ruler in Mark 10 that the object of our affection must be God alone. What do we treasure more than God? What do we hold onto more than God? What pulls us away from God? What do we trust in more than God? We may think that these questions are easy to answer. Now imagine Jesus telling you to sell everything you have, give it away, and follow him. Would you go away sad, or do you find yourself being liberal in your generosity?

Second, do we know God more than we know anything else? Do we value his word in our lives? Do we meditate on it? Does our heart break at the things that break the things of God? Do we put a premium on thinking on the things of God? "Finally, brothers, whatever is true, whatever is honorable, whatever is just, whatever is pure, whatever is lovely, whatever is commendable, if there is any excellence, if there is anything worthy of praise, think about these things" (Phil. 4:8).

Third, do we strive to build up those around us? Do we value others more than ourselves? Do we seek the interests of others before our own? Our love for others will flow from our love for him. Do other people hold a priority for you? Is their spiritual well-being of paramount concern?

> Therefore if you have any encouragement from being united with Christ, if any comfort from his love, if any common sharing in the Spirit, if any tenderness and compassion, then make my joy complete by being likeminded, having the same love, being one in spirit and of one mind. Do nothing out of selfish ambition or vain conceit. Rather, in humility value others above yourselves, not looking to your own interests but each of you to the interests of the others. In your relationships with one another, have the same mindset as Christ Jesus … (Phil. 2:1–5)

These are tough questions indeed. But they provide insight into our hearts. You see, the degree to which we love our neighbor tells us something about our love for God himself. If you find and see the impossibility in the questions above and the command of Christ, if you realize that you are not able to keep those commands even for one second, take heart. Jesus did it for you. He gives you the grace and strength to learn how to live this way. He provides the mercy/forgiveness to move forward when we find we have failed.

My prayer for you today is for eyes to see the brokenness around you, ears to hear the hurt, hands to help bear the burdens of others, and feet eager to move toward it all. I also pray for a heart that loves, treasures, seeks, and pursues the kingdom of God and its righteousness. Grace for the journey.

The Affections of a Workman Approved

> But as for you, continue in what you have learned and have firmly believed, knowing from whom you learned it and how from childhood you have been acquainted with the sacred writings, which are able to make you wise for salvation through faith in Christ Jesus. All Scripture is breathed out by God and profitable for teaching, for reproof, for correction, and for training in righteousness, that the man of God[b] may be complete, equipped for every good work.
>
> —2 Timothy 3:14–17

In speaking about becoming a workman approved and the path of a workman approved, Paul writes to Timothy about the loves of the heart and how by seeing the affections of a person's life you can tell who owns their heart. Are they a workman approved or one deceived by the loves of the lures of this world? What did Jesus mean, after all, when he said "follow me"?

Know this: the path of a workman approved is driven by, is rooted in, finds its beginning, and ends in Christ and what he has done for you. This is critical to understand. You cannot manufacture the path of a workman approved. You can try and might even deceive those in the church and yourself that you are on the path of the workman approved. Over the next few pages, let's consider the idea of a workman approved.

First, Paul begins this section of his letter to Timothy by talking about misplaced affections with this phrase, "But understand this." This is more than just an instruction for what is to follow but very much a link to what he just finished saying. In 2 Timothy 2, Paul encourages Timothy to "Do your best to present yourself to God as one approved, a worker who has no need to be ashamed, rightly handling the word of truth." He wants Timothy to not lose heart, be deceived, or become sidetracked and thus shipwreck his faith. He wants Timothy to know that even as he seeks the peace and purity of the church through the gospel, there will be those who do not. And so, he warns him that "in the last days there will be times of difficulty."

To be clear, this phrase, "in the last days," is frequently misunderstood in our day. Paul was not talking about some time in the distance that Timothy would not see. When scripture refers to the last days, it simply talks about the time between Christ's first and second coming. I want to be clear here. I'm referring to the whole time between the first and second coming, not just the period right before his return. So from our vantage point, what Paul wants Timothy to understand, he wants us to understand as well. For in our time, just as in his and just as in the time to come, there will be times of difficulty. There will be weeds that grow within the harvest. There will be wheat with the chaff. There will be wolves in the midst of the sheep. We must understand this and be on the lookout. We must rightly handle the word of truth and present ourselves to God as one approved and unashamed.

Paul is not talking about those outside the church in this passage. One would think, reading through this list, that is exactly who he was taking aim. He wasn't. We are to be on the lookout for those within the church who are "lovers of self," "lovers of money," and "lovers of pleasure." These are the loves of this world. These were at the heart of the temptation. They are antithetical to the love of God and love of others and are contrary to the gospel.

Jesus referred to the loves of this world as the world, the flesh, and the devil in the parable of the sower. John referred to them as the desires of the flesh, the desires of the eyes, and the pride of life. Those who place such a high value on these loves find themselves, as this passage states, being "proud, arrogant, abusive, disobedient to their parents, ungrateful, unholy, heartless, unappeasable, slanderous, without self-control, brutal, not loving good, treacherous, reckless, swollen with conceit … having the appearance of godliness, but denying its power."

We see in our time, as in times past, the lure of the loves of this world. From the accumulation of stuff to coveting to our own boasting and complaining, we demonstrate to a watching world a complete lack of grace.

Paul contrasts the love of this world with the love of God. To be a lover of this world is to not be a lover of God. You cannot serve two masters. The love of this world does not share a bed with the love of God. The lack of contentment doesn't coexist with the rest found in the Sabbath of our Lord. The pursuit of things leading to destruction finds its end not in things eternal. You cannot hold the hand of Satan and the hand of the Lord. You must make a choice. What holds your attention? What do you truly treasure?

Today if you hear his voice, turn to him with love and affection and discover the peace that comes from knowing him.

The Path of a Workman Approved

But as for you, continue in what you have learned and have firmly believed, knowing from whom you learned it and how from childhood you have been acquainted with the sacred writings, which are able to make you wise for salvation through faith in Christ Jesus. All Scripture is breathed out by God and profitable for teaching, for reproof, for correction, and for training in righteousness, that the man of God[b] may be complete, equipped for every good work.

—2 Timothy 3:14–17

In the previous section, we looked at a workman approved and where they place their affections. Once your affections are set, once your motivations are set, where or how do you go? This brings us to the second point of this passage. What characterizes the path of a workman approved? First, a workman approved listens to his word. This comes from reading scripture, meditating upon it, and obeying his word. Paul said this to Timothy, "But as for you, continue in what you have learned and have firmly believed, knowing from whom you learned it and how from childhood you have been acquainted with the sacred writings, which are able to make you wise for salvation through faith in Christ Jesus." Scripture reminds us:

- "Man shall not live by bread alone but by every word that proceeds from the mouth of God." (Matt. 4:4)
- "Your word is a lamp to my feet and a light to my path." (Ps. 119:105)

- "How can a young man keep his way pure? By guarding it according to your word. With my whole heart I seek you; let me not wander from your commandments! I have stored up your word in my heart, that I might not sin against you." (Ps 119:9–11)
- "In the way of your testimonies, I delight as much as in all riches. I will meditate on your precepts and fix my eyes on your ways. I will delight in your statutes; I will not forget your word." (Ps. 119:14–16)

The path of a workman approved starts with listening to his word. This isn't just a casual opening of his word. Paul indicates how from childhood Timothy was "acquainted with the sacred writings." His life was built upon the word of God. Paul doesn't stop there, though. Just because Timothy had been well acquainted with scripture since his youth, it was no reason to stop or set aside the treasuring of God's word. Paul commands Timothy to "continue in what you have learned and firmly believed."

The same is true for us. Do we treasure God's word as a guiding lamp unto our feet? Do we store up his word in our hearts that we might not sin against him? Do we delight in his word? Is it something we meditate upon? The path of a workman approved begins in the word of God. A workman approved is well acquainted with scripture and continues to study it. RC Sproul, in commenting on this passage in his book, *Knowing Scripture*, writes,

> The Christian who is not diligently involved in a serious study of Scripture is simply inadequate as a disciple of Christ. To be an adequate Christian and competent in the things of God one must do more than attend "sharing sessions" and "bless-me parties." We cannot learn competency by osmosis. The biblically illiterate Christian is not only inadequate but unequipped.[1]

Second, a workman approved understands that obedience is a transformed life, not a list of dos and don'ts observed. Paul puts it this way in our passage, "All Scripture is breathed out by God and profitable for teaching, for reproof, for correction, and for training in righteousness, that the man of God may be complete, equipped for every good work." Salvation leads to a restored relationship with God and a new life. It is through teaching, reproof, correction, and training in righteousness that we see transformation.

Notice, he calls scripture profitable. The life he leads you to is advantageous to you, profitable, and good. It is not a list of dos and don'ts. Rather, it is a lifestyle that stems from a changed heart.

This is what we see in 1 Corinthians 13. If you read through the chapter, you will see how love is described, not as a list of adjectives but as verbs and actions. It is not a one-time event but a way of life. It is driven by what Christ has done on our behalf.

That is what we see in Exodus 20. The whole of the Ten Commandments was never intended to be a checklist. Rather, it was designed for us, in response to what God has done for us, to ask questions like, "If I am not to steal, then what should I do? Do I hold on too tightly to the things of this world? Do I fail to give to God what is his? When I see my neighbor in need and I have what they need, do I turn away or gladly open my hand? Am I uncomfortable amidst the poor and needy? Or do I welcome them with open arms?"

Third, a workman approved learns and works in the community. Paul writes, "But as for you, continue in what you have learned and have firmly believed, knowing from whom you learned it." There is a clear picture of not living and learning and working alone in the work God has for his people. At the start of the letter, he says, "I am reminded of your sincere faith, which first lived in your grandmother Lois and in your mother Eunice and, I am persuaded, now lives in you also." And again, "Rather, join with me in suffering for the gospel, by the power of God. He has saved us and called us to a holy life—not because of anything we have done but because of his own purpose and grace." The writer of Hebrews exhorts his readers not to abandon the regular gathering of believers. Scripture is full of "one another" statements that point to life in the faith being life in community. Indeed, a workman approved learns and works in the community.

Fourth, a workman approved has work to do. Paul wrote to Timothy, "All Scripture is breathed out by God and profitable for teaching, for reproof, for correction, and for training in righteousness, that the man of God may be complete, equipped for every good work." In his letter to the Ephesians, Paul writes, "For by grace you have been saved through faith. And this is not your own doing; it is the gift of God, not a result of works, so that no one may boast. For we are his workmanship, created in Christ Jesus for good works, which God prepared beforehand, that we should walk in them."

Finally, Christ alone makes you a workman approved. Being a workman approved has nothing to do with you, what you do, or what you have done. It has everything to do with the person and work of Christ. It has everything to do with what Jesus did for you. Paul says to Timothy in this passage, "But as for you, continue in what you have learned and have firmly believed, knowing from whom you learned it and how from childhood you have been acquainted with the sacred writings, which are able to make you wise for salvation through faith in Christ Jesus." Paul states in Romans that the gospel is the power of God for the salvation of everyone who believes (Rom. 1:16). Solomon wrote that the fear of the Lord is the beginning of wisdom (Prov. 9:10). James said in his letter that if anyone lacks wisdom, he should ask God, who gives generously to all without finding fault and that it would be given to him (James 1:5).

Dear reader, it is "by grace you have been saved through faith. And this is not your own doing; it is the gift of God, not a result of works, so that no one may boast. For we are his workmanship, created in Christ Jesus for good works, which God prepared beforehand, that we should walk in them" (Eph. 2:8–10). A true faith is a living faith. Salvation is not about some prayer prayed or an aisle walked. It is about faith alone in Christ alone, according to scripture alone to the glory of God alone. So being a workman approved is about a rightly placed affection granted by the King.

Who or what do you believe in? If Christ does not hold the only place, repent and call upon Christ as Lord and Savior. Believe that he was indeed raised from the dead. Begin to live with that in mind. Cling to the gospel, for it is "able to make you wise for salvation through faith in Christ Jesus."

Are You Ready?

But concerning that day or that hour, no one knows, not even the angels in heaven, nor the Son, but only the Father.

—Mark 13:32

As we consider the parable of the tenants in Mark 12 and the teaching on the destruction of the temple in Mark 13, we need to see that they both point to the same thing, the destruction of the temple. In Mark 13, we see Jesus sitting on the Mount of Olives opposite the temple. We see the same thing in the story at the end of chapter 12 where Jesus sat opposite the treasury. In both cases, Jesus sat in judgment, telling the people that the object of their faith was nothing. What does Jesus tell us within this section as he pronounces judgment on the temple and the people who put their faith in the temple?

First, God's grace extends to all people, not just Israel. As such, he has given us the responsibility, the privilege, and the awesome job of sharing the gospel of Jesus to the whole world. From Matthew 28:18–20 and Romans 10:14–15, we understand the job before us. There is no plan B. This is God's plan. You need to ask yourself how seriously you take the call.

Second, we need to live lives that demonstrate we are ready for his coming. This point is really what is at the heart of the eschatological passages, not God's people trying to figure out if Jesus will come today, tomorrow, next week, or next year. The parable of the ten virgins, among others that Jesus taught, drives this home. If he can come like a thief in the night, would we rather him find us about the work of the kingdom (preaching the gospel) or trying to pinpoint that return (which really has no value considering Christ himself doesn't seek to know)?

Third, we need to look forward to that day with joyous anticipation, knowing that all that is wrong and broken will be fixed, what is sick and diseased will be made whole, and injustice and suffering will be made right. The second coming of our gracious Lord and Savior, Jesus, like the sword of Damocles, should drive us to prayer, move us to action, perk up our attitudes, and set our path/direction. We should want to be found with an attitude that matches a life ready for his coming.

May our passion be centered on being ready, not an endless pursuit of something we will never know. His coming will be like a thief in the night. Be ready as you would for even that event. Grace for the journey.

Radical Change (Part 1)

Therefore, since we are surrounded by such a great cloud of witnesses, let us throw off everything that hinders and the sin that so easily entangles. And let us run with perseverance the race marked out for us, fixing our eyes on Jesus, the pioneer and perfecter of faith.

—Hebrews 12:1–2

The picture is one of the Olympic sporting events: a great arena filled with people, athletes on the field preparing for the race before them, and the crowd cheering them on to persevere and win the race marked out for them. It's a thrilling picture indeed, one not just for the Olympics but for life.

One of the phrases that we proclaim in the Apostles' Creed is that we believe in the "communion of saints." The great crowd of witnesses, both living and dead, fill the arena and shout their encouragement to us who are running the race. In some cases, we are running. In others, we are cheering. We have a role to play, and it is our duty to persevere in that role.

Years ago, I spent time teaching high school students about the heroes of the faith. We marched through history learning about faith, what it looks like and what it does. We studied

- Abraham and learned the components of true salvific faith and the object of our faith;

- Joseph and discovered the faithfulness of faith and what it means to trust completely in God's providence no matter the cost;
- Ruth and saw the humbleness, beauty, and industry of faith;
- Esther and experienced the courage of faith;
- the lives of the early church leaders and considered the perseverance of faith;
- the death of Polycarp and witnessed the confidence of faith;
- the life of George Mueller and observed the trust of faith; and
- the adventures of Brother Andrew and saw the mission and vision of faith.

Frequently when we look at others who are impacting the world, we have a tendency to say, "These were/are great men and women of faith. They changed the world. I don't have faith that big. I can't change the world like they did" or "They were leaders. I am not a leader." And so we quit. We give up on trying to change the world and focus on what fun we could have.

This is not just shallow thinking. It is shallow Christianity. By allowing these thoughts to creep into our lives and actions, we reject not only the sovereignty of God but his power to change lives and events for his glory. We forget that Christ can do anything with anybody at any time and in any place he wants. James 5:17–18 tells us, "Elijah was a human being, even as we are. He prayed earnestly that it would not rain, and it did not rain on the land for three and a half years. Again he prayed, and the heavens gave rain, and the earth produced its crops."

I asked the students what the main focus of this passage was. They naturally focused on the action Elijah took, prayer, which was important. However, they missed the most important message James had: great men and women of faith were persons just like you and me, and God can and will change the world for his honor and glory using individuals like you and me.

My encouragement to you today is this:

1. Stop comparing yourself to others as the standard for whether you can impact the world for Christ.
2. Fix your eyes on Jesus, the author and perfecter of your faith and the one who will provide.
3. Run the race Jesus has marked out for you with faith that demonstrates courage, humility, industry, and all those other traits associated with it.

Grace for the journey.

Radical Change (Part 2)

Therefore, since we are surrounded by such a great cloud of witnesses, let us throw off everything that hinders and the sin that so easily entangles. And let us run with perseverance the race marked out for us, fixing our eyes on Jesus, the pioneer and perfecter of faith.

—Hebrews 12:1–2

I spoke at a youth gathering years ago and talked about overcoming shallow thinking and shallow Christianity in order to make a change for Christ. I asked if they had heard of a man named Gideon. Most in the room had heard of him, which was good considering they had grown up in the church. One of the students raised their hand, I called on them, and they proceeded to tell me about the great victory he had over the Midianites. With three hundred people, he beat an army of tens of thousands, an amazing and truly an inspiring story, a story only God could have written and accomplished.

I shocked them when I said they only told the glamorous part of the story. I then proceeded to outline a different picture of Gideon, a man who was mentioned in Hebrews 11, a man who was just like us. The Gideon I introduced to them in Judges 6 was afraid (6:11, 27, 7:10); had no confidence (6:13); was not strong (6:15); and was hesitant/doubtful (6:17, 36). He put confidence in numbers and human strength rather than God (7:2). It's truly a different picture than we tend to remember but more realistic to what I look like. Despite these, God used his small faith, multiplied it to obedience, and performed a great work in saving his people.

Let's consider how God might move our hearts in faith and obedience. For example, Philippians 2:12–13 tells us, "Therefore, my dear friends, as you have always obeyed—not only in my presence, but now much more in my absence—continue to work out your salvation with fear and trembling, for it is God who works in you to will and to act in order to fulfill his good purpose."

What does Paul commend the church for? "You have always obeyed." How does Paul commend them? "not only … but now much more." When did they do these good works? "[I]n my absence." Who did they rely on for the ability to do these hard things? "[F]or it is God who works in you." These Christians were zealous to obey God not just in front of folks but in private as well. They did it in love and relied on the strength of Christ to carry out the mission.

Sound familiar? Hebrews 10:24 says, "And let us consider how we may spur one another on toward love and good deeds." The author of Hebrews says, "And let us consider." What should we be spending our time thinking about? "[H]ow we may spur one another on."

Having a spirit of encouragement, we should be thinking about how we can build each other up in the Lord, how we can bear one another's burdens, and how we can love one another better. This is a radical thought process. Who should we be looking to encourage? "[O]ne another." To what end do we encourage? "[T]oward love and good deeds."

What are these types of actions? Paul gives us a hint to this in 1 Timothy 4:12 when he writes, "Don't let anyone look down on you because you are young, but set an example for the believers in speech, in conduct, in love, in faith and in purity." Is this easy? No, but life is about doing hard things.

Finally, Paul says in Colossians 3:17, "And whatever you do, whether in word or deed, do it all in the name of the Lord Jesus, giving thanks to God the Father through him." Is there a limit to what is commanded here? No, Paul says very clearly, "whatever you do." What is the scope of the command? "[W]ord or deed." This covers thoughts as well since they are the genesis of both words and deeds. So the scope is quite complete. How is it to be done? "[I]n the name of the Lord Jesus."

Why is this significant? You are not doing it for yourself. You are not acting in your name or for yourself. You are acting in the name of someone else, the Lord Jesus. When you have this in mind, it just might change how you react. How are we to carry out the command? "[G]iving thanks to God the Father." A thankful heart drives a grateful attitude that moves a person, just like you and me, to action.

My encouragement to you today is from Hebrews 12:1–2, "Therefore, since we are surrounded by such a great cloud of witnesses, let us throw off everything that hinders and the sin that so easily entangles. And let us run with perseverance the race marked out for us, fixing our eyes on Jesus, the pioneer and perfecter of faith." Look to Jesus. Walk with Jesus. Rest in Jesus. Grace for the journey.

I Am the Resurrection and the Life ... Do You Believe This?

> After saying these things, he said to them, "Our friend Lazarus has fallen asleep, but I go to awaken him."
>
> —John 11:11

Jesus told us that we would face heartache, suffering, pain, and death as part of life. In this story, we see one of Jesus's best friends dying. We see the pain experienced by Mary and Martha. We see the compassion of Christ in the midst of it all. As I consider this passage, I ask, "How should we face pain and suffering and death?" This passage gives us some insights into that as part of the narrative leading up to the crucifixion, as Jesus is on his way to Jerusalem, where he would suffer and die for the sins of his people.

One of the first things we do when we face heartache, struggles, or death is to try to find a reason for it. The challenge is that most of the time, we don't find one. However, one thing we can rest in and be confident of is God's sovereignty and the fact that everything that comes to pass will bring glory to Him. We see that in verse 4, "it is for God's glory so that God's son may be glorified through it."

When I think about losing two fathers, living in pain every day for thirty-plus years, almost losing my son, losing my job, and others, I cannot tell you the reason why I walked through each. I can, however, tell you that I take peace and solace in the fact that God is sovereign and that not even a sparrow falls to the ground without his knowledge. Being of much greater value than the sparrow, I know God cares for me even in the midst of trials. In looking at this passage, we can clearly see a role to play as Christians and a proper response. In no particular order, let me walk you through what I see and what has brought me encouragement.

The first thing is his grace is sufficient. What is meant by "his grace is sufficient"? Sufficiency can actually be translated as contentment. Being content in his grace brings peace, no condemnation, hope, comfort, confidence, and a purpose that looks beyond the trouble to the redemption that lies ahead. It means we do not let trouble rule who we are and our attitudes. It doesn't mean that we don't mourn. It specifically points to our Comforter and the fact that we rest in him, not our troubles.

The second thing is that Jesus listened with love and compassion to both Mary and Martha (verses 21 and 32). As Christians, we are to listen, hug, and love those who are hurting. We are to seek out those who are hurting.

The third thing is that Jesus was moved with compassion. Verse 33 says that when he saw her weeping, he was deeply moved. As Christians, we need to be moved with compassion toward those who are hurting. This means we have to have eyes to see it around us. Jesus was good at that. Scripture is full of the fact that "Jesus saw."

The fourth thing is that it is ok to mourn. Verse 35 tells us that Jesus wept. It is ok to mourn. But it is not ok to let the mourning process consume you. God is bigger than any trouble you face.

The fifth thing is that it is ok to be angry. Jesus was angry at sin and the effects of sin. In verse 38, we see Jesus "deeply moved." The Greek word here indicates more of a righteous anger than just being moved emotionally. He was angry at sin, its effects, and its result. He did something about it. "Roll the stone away," he says to us. "You will see God glorified," he reminds us. We should ask ourselves, "Are you angry at sin, its effects, and its results? What are you doing about it?"

The final thing is that Jesus remained resolute in his focus on setting the captives free (verse 8). He marched with an eye to Calvary. The ever-present trouble of pain, suffering, and death should drive us to share the gospel with those around us. Not knowing when, where, or how people will face it, we should not hoard the gospel to ourselves. Pain, suffering, and death are hard. However, Christ is bigger than each and offers hope, peace, and comfort to all who turn to him. Nowhere did he promise to take away those troubles. But Jesus promised to never leave us or forsake us. That is a promise worth holding on to.

My hope is that you gain encouragement from it and hand over those things that weigh you down, knowing that he will carry you through all of it. When you do, when you experience the compassion of the King, you will in turn demonstrate that compassion to those around you going through trouble. In doing so, perhaps you will turn many to life through faith in Jesus. "Meanwhile a large crowd of Jews found out that Jesus was there and came, not only because of him but also to see Lazarus, whom he had raised from the dead. So the chief priests made plans to kill Lazarus as well, *for on account of him many of the Jews were going over to Jesus and believing in him*" (John 12:9–11).

Christ's Death, Your Gain

Do not be alarmed. You seek Jesus of Nazareth, who was crucified. He has risen; he is not here.

—Mark 16:6

For to me, to live is Christ and to die is gain.

—Philippians 1:21

As we move to the end of the book of Mark, we are confronted with the death, burial, and resurrection of Jesus. Paul tells the Philippians that in Christ there is gain. That gain is seen in the many promises secured in eternity past by his faithfulness.

- "Therefore, there is now no condemnation for those who are in Christ Jesus." (Rom. 8:1)
- "And we know that in all things God works for the good of those who love him, who have been called according to his purpose." (Rom. 8:28)
- "If God is for us, who can be against us?" (Rom. 8:31b)
- "He who did not spare his own Son, but gave him up for us all—how will he not also, along with him, graciously give us all things?" (Rom. 8:32)
- "Who shall separate us from the love of Christ?" (Rom. 8:35)

Through the life, death, and resurrection of Christ, we have freedom from the power of sin; freedom from guilt; comfort that in God's sovereignty, our trials will work for our good; freedom from the accuser; confidence that our defense is sure and our position in Christ secure; freedom from the worry and fear of death because our eternal home awaits us; and freedom from worry knowing that if God did not spare even his son for us that the owner of "the cattle on a thousand hills" (Ps. 50:10) would provide our very needs.

As I write this, I have been suffering from depression, more specifically, feeling completely alone. I have felt dismissed and feeling as though I am nothing. I have wondered if anyone cared. As a result, I felt angry. What these passages teach me is that I can be free from that depression and anger—free to walk away from it, reject it, and be free from it. Scripture reminds me that:

- I am not alone; I can never be separated from God and his love.
- I am not alone; in him, I have brothers, mothers, fathers, and sisters a thousand times over.
- I am not alone; in him, I am a son and heir.
- I am not alone; in his sovereignty, he holds my future and provides what is needed.
- I am not alone; in his love, he provided another Comforter who stands with me in strength.

The promise and the hope found in what Christ did on my behalf on the cross provide purpose to life, promise in suffering, and the prize of eternal life with him. And it means I am not alone. Christ screamed on the cross, "My God, my God, why have you forsaken me!" so I would never be forsaken. To me, to live is Christ, and to die is gain.

Meeting Jesus on the Road to Emmaus: A Personal Journey

While they were talking and discussing together, Jesus himself drew near and went with them. But their eyes were kept from recognizing him.
—Luke 24:15–16

This last chapter is meant to be different. It is more than just a look at a Bible story. I see it as a personal journey. I wrote this during one of those dark nights of the soul. I wanted to share it with you to give you a peek into my heart. Excuse the length. My hope is that you will hear what I learned as I journeyed on my own road to Emmaus.

The story takes place on a dusty road leading out of Jerusalem, heading west-northwest of the city. It was a seven-mile walk. At a normal pace, it might take two to three hours to traverse. Here, we find two of Jesus's disciples. Scripture only names one of them, Cleopas, a disciple who followed Jesus, one who now found himself disappointed, scared, confused, and wondering where God was in all of this. Their hopes were dashed. They were wondering about the years spent following Jesus and whether they had been in vain.

I can understand these feelings: being scared, confused, disappointed, and wondering where God was in the midst of it all. Back in 1999, when my wife was pregnant with our son, Jerry, we received word that he would not live. The pregnancy had gone horribly wrong. I was crushed and devastated beyond measure. When he defied all odds and was born, the doctors declared everything to be wrong with him, but they never could pinpoint what it was. Time and time again, we had to take Jerry to the emergency room and the doctor's office. Multiple body casts, a harness that kept him from crawling, and one illness after another, it was emotionally draining.

Through it all, God was demonstrating his grace and mercy, providing community to come alongside us to care for our girls while I worked, connections to Shriner hospitals to care for our son at no cost to us, and family a thousand times over to give us hugs.

Despite these graces, I still wondered where God was. My hopes were dashed as the normalcy of a newborn boy was replaced with struggle after struggle. As a father, as a man, I was hit with my inability to fix it. That alone crushed me. I remember one night holding my son. I was weeping as he was sick again. I knew we would need to take him to the hospital again. There was nothing I could do. I cried out that night to God that if taking my life would fix my son, I would gladly give it. I could not bear it anymore. That night and in that prayer, I thought like I was talking to the walls. Where was God? Why the silence? Looking back on that time, I see now God's grace and the gospel being shown to me in the depths of my despair. I see similarities to this story on the road to Emmaus.

I see three things as part of this story that provide me with great comfort in the gospel:

1. Jesus draws near to me even when I am not seeking after him.
2. My view of Jesus informs how I face trouble.
3. My response to Jesus when I hear his voice results in a change of heart.

All about this story is flooded by the grace, mercy, kindness, and gentleness of our Lord toward his people. It should give us great comfort as we rest in his gospel. But let's get back to our story.

These two men had heard the scuttlebutt, the women who went to the tomb and were greeted by its emptiness and an angel proclaiming his resurrection, Peter and John running to the tomb, finding it empty, and the rumblings of some seeing and talking to Jesus. Even though they discounted the stories, they still marveled at them, and as they walked, they were discussing all that had happened.

At this point, Jesus drew near to them. We see this in verse 15—what I want you to see in this verse is something so very dear to me—that Jesus draws near even when we are not seeking him. This is our first point of grace. Even when we are not looking for him, even when we are not seeking him, and even when we might be running away from him, as Jonah did, Christ pursues us in grace, mercy, and gentleness. As Isaiah declared, "A bruised reed he will not break."

To be a follower of Jesus in the days around the crucifixion was dangerous. We see Peter on Thursday night/Friday morning denying his best friend because he was afraid. We see the followers of Jesus locking themselves in their homes. All were fearful. So it would not have been unusual for these two to quiet their conversation when someone they did not know came up alongside them during their walk to Emmaus. Rather than being rude or dismissive, they show kindness to the stranger when he asks what they were talking about. After all, everyone in Jerusalem would have known what had happened that weekend. The whole city had yelled, "Crucify him!" And now as they left the city, one man came alongside them and asked what they were talking about, what had just happened. He acted as if he didn't know anything that had just transpired. Their question somewhat shows astonishment and amazement by asking, "Are you the only one?" There was no rudeness in it as they continued to speak with this man.

But Jesus pressed them on their faith. Jesus was always concerned about the faith of his people: the giving of faith, the building up of faith, and the strengthening of faith. We see this throughout the Gospels, no less so than when Jesus raised Lazarus from the grave. Jesus was glad for the trial. Scripture tells us because it served for the strengthening of the faith of the apostles and the family and for giving faith to others. We see this in John 11:14, 26, 40, and 45. And so we see Jesus pressing these two on the road about their faith. "What things?" he said. His goal was to build up their faith.

But Jesus pressed them in order to encourage and comfort them. Jesus could see much sadness in their countenance. It was so evident that even a stranger looking at them could tell that they were sad. This almost seemed like a fulfillment of what Jesus said in Mark 2:19–20, doesn't it? "And Jesus said to them, 'Can the wedding guests fast while the bridegroom is with them? As long as they have the bridegroom with them, they cannot fast. The days will come when the bridegroom is taken away from them, and then they will fast in that day.'"

Jesus, through this interaction, would restore gladness to their souls and remind them again of what God had said regarding the coming of the Messiah. Glory be to the one who loves us even when we do not love him, who seeks after us even when we do not seek after him, who teaches us even when we have been so dense as to ignore everything taught over the many years to that point. He is indeed our shepherd in whom we find all we need. We see the shepherd of Psalm 23 coming alongside these men in their distress. Listen again to those words, "He makes me lie down in green pastures. He leads me beside still waters. He restores my soul. He leads me in paths of righteousness for his name's sake. Even though I walk through the valley of the shadow of death, I will fear no evil, for you are with me; your rod and your staff, they comfort me."

Hear the words: he makes me, he leads me, and he restores all for one purpose, his name's sake. His rod and staff and his word comfort me. That is the picture of the Good Shepherd as he graciously pursues these two men on the road to Emmaus. That is the picture of our Good Shepherd as he graciously pursues us on our road to Emmaus.

This brings me to the second point. How we view him will inform how we respond to trouble. As the men answer Jesus's question, we see great insight into what they thought of Jesus, where their faith was. Listen to the words they used in verses 19, 20, and 21.

- "A man who was a prophet …"
- "Mighty in deed and word …"

- "We had hoped he was the one to redeem Israel ..."
- "And besides all this, it is now the third day ..."

It is almost like a newspaper article how they relay the events of the day to this stranger. What is this reminiscent of? In Mark 8, Jesus asked the disciples, "Who do men say that I the Son of Man am?" They answered in much the same way, John the Baptist, Elijah, or one of the other prophets. Then he asked, "Who do you say that I am?" Peter replied, "You are the Christ, the Son of the Living God." There is no hope for us if he were just another prophet. Now as the Christ, the Son of the Living God, that rock, that declaration the church has been built on for all time.

How does our view of who he is impact how we face troubles and trials, even blessings and prosperity? If we see him only as some prophet or moral teacher, we are most to be pitied as we rest our hope upon nothing. But if we see him as the Christ, the Son of the Living God, the creator and sustainer of all things, sovereign over all things, holding all things in his hand so that not even a molecule or atom runs rogue, well, that is a rock that not even the gates of hell can prevail against. Trials and troubles might come, but that rock, that confession of faith, stands unmoved, unshaken, and secure.

Listen again to the psalmist, "Even though I walk through the valley of the shadow of death, I will fear no evil." Why would he not fear even death? Why would it not matter if he were in a building and planes flew into it, cutting off all escape? "[F]or you are with me."

In Psalm 18, we read,

> With the merciful you show yourself merciful; with the blameless man you show yourself blameless; with the purified you show yourself pure; and with the crooked you make yourself seem tortuous. For you save a humble people, but the haughty eyes you bring down. For it is you who light my lamp; the LORD my God lightens my darkness. For by you I can run against a troop, and by my God I can leap over a

wall. This God—his way is perfect; the word of the LORD proves true; he is a shield for all those who take refuge in him.

The questions we have to ask is, "Is our Christ too small?" and "Is our gospel too small?" If we want to find peace and rest in the midst of trouble, confidence in the face of death, joy in the face of loss, and generosity and community in the midst of plenty, all we need to do is draw near to Jesus, who is drawing near to you in your day of trouble and in your day of plenty. This is what I had to learn as I walked through my desert, my valley of despair.

When we see him for who he is, we are more than conquerors because we are in him. Our hearts are revived because we then know that nothing can separate us from his love, that nothing can pull us from the Father's grip, and that all hell can throw at the people of God is but nothing compared to the greatness and power of Jesus the Christ. In that, we can take comfort, and our sorrow can be turned to joy, knowing our King has conquered the grave and secured our salvation for all time.

This leads to my final observation. What should our response be? Moving along the story, we see Jesus reproving them for their lack of faith. He said in verse 25, "O foolish ones." They were foolish because they believed something that was detrimental to their very soul, that Christ had not been raised from the dead. They were foolish because they were slow to faith, that when things got hard, they let go of the things that mattered. They were slow to believe even the prophets from centuries earlier who had written that the Son of Man must die and rise again. In his mercy, he doesn't leave them with the reproof. He corrects them, doesn't he? For our Savior is a loving King who rights our paths and sets us again on our journey. He said to them in verse 26, "Was it not necessary" and again in verse 27, "And beginning with Moses and all the prophets he interpreted to them in all the Scriptures." He reproves them and corrects them.

What happens next should give us great hope and encouragement.

We see a drawing near again in verse 28, this time to a place. They drew near to the place they were staying. Jesus tested their faith again, as we see in verse 28, "he acted as if he were going farther."

But the disciples found their faith strengthened. They urged him strongly to stay. This brings me to the first application. When we hear the word of God, do we strongly urge him to stay close? Do our hearts burn within us for him? Are we so focused on programs, the delivery of the message, the person teaching that we miss the gospel? When we sit in church each week, do our hearts burn within us for him as we listen to his word?

We see his grace again when he went in and stayed with them. When he broke the bread and said a prayer, they saw him for who he was. Do we, when the Lord's Supper is served, see the one who bore our sins? Do we see our hope? This is where the means of grace builds up our faith in him through that sacrament.

At that moment, they were changed. They repented. "[D]id not our hearts burn within us while he talked to us?" They rose that same hour. They returned to Jerusalem, seven miles to Emmaus and seven miles back. They couldn't get back quickly enough. Their hearts went from utter despair to leaping for joy. Their countenance changed. We see that upon their return in verse 35, "They told them what had happened." Does our countenance change when we enter his courts, when we come to worship him?

Recently, as I was driving to Purdue University, I came upon an accident. What was truly horrific was the coroner's vehicle driving alongside me to that scene. As I passed by the scene, I saw a car crushed beyond measure. There was no driver's side anymore. There was no driver. As I thought of this, I was reminded that as an elder, I will not be judged on that day for whether I got the budget of the church right, if we had this or that program running, or if everything we did was so clearly wrapped around some mission statement. No, what I will be held accountable for are the souls of those entrusted to me. Did I preach Christ and him crucified? Did I preach the resurrection? Did I proclaim the life-giving, reconciliation-granting, hope-filling words of the gospel to you daily? Did I love you well in that? Christ's example in this story should be mine. But not just mine, yours as well.

Returning to my story at the beginning, like these men, I carried a sad face. But you see it was in the gospel preached to me by Christ through his people that once again brought a smile to my face. For in the gospel, the alienation we have toward God, each other, and even ourselves is turned to a great and mighty reconciliation.

Do you know that life eternal? Do you know that reconciliation? Do you have that hope? If not, you can find it in him today. Don't leave this chapter without being confronted by Jesus. He gives us the grace we need for today; he gives the hope we desire for tomorrow and the confidence of eternity with him. Draw near to the one who draws near to you and find his peace and grace for the journey.

Epilogue: Discovering Jesus Through Life

Now to him who is able to keep you from stumbling and to present you blameless before the presence of his glory with great joy, to the only God, our Savior, through Jesus Christ our Lord, be glory, majesty, dominion, and authority, before all time and now and forever. Amen.

—Jude 24–25

Throughout these pages, you have heard me say with confidence to trust him no matter the circumstance, to live with peace and joy in the midst of it all. I am sure you have thought the following, "You don't know what my life has been like," "I lost my job," "I have lost everything," "Sickness eats away at my very existence," and "There is no hope!" In the midst of even that despair, I can say, "Have faith, and persevere in patience, hope, and joy." I say this knowing the pain and suffering in those words.

Many years ago, I faced similar troubles in my family. Cancer began to eat away at my father. My brother was suffering from kidney failure. My son was given a death sentence even before he was born. I have suffered from chronic pain for almost thirty years. Yet in that season of life, the gospel's application became clear in my mind. I realized that if the gospel is true, the future is certain and true and good. Romans 8 reminds us, "we know that in all things God works for the good of those who love him, who have been called according to his purpose."

Practically speaking, what does this mean? From the standpoint of my son, I realized that if God, in his infinite grace and mercy, chose to let my son live, I would have a lifetime of memories with him here on earth and an eternity of memories with him in heaven. If God, in his infinite grace and mercy, chose to take my son, I would have an eternity of memories with him in heaven. No bitterness, just trust and confidence in the one who holds all things together in his hands. Whatever the decision, I know his goodness is complete, and even though it might be tough, I trust his provision through the good and bad of either outcome.

Where are things at? My son has a master's degree and works in Texas. This one whom the doctors wanted to kill is a child of the living God, seeking first his kingdom and his righteousness, even if imperfectly. He is a man with a gentle spirit and kind heart. He loves to pester his sisters but would gladly give his life for them. The road wasn't always easy, but the gospel gives grace sufficient along the way to meet life's challenges.

Whether things turn out the way we want them or not, trust Christ for the outcome and live in the light of that faith. Discover Jesus. Life with him will give meaning and purpose, hope and direction, and life abundant. Life may throw bumps along the way, but life with Christ is better. It is incomparable to anything else, even when walking through the valley of the shadow of death. Will you join me on the journey?

Notes

All Scripture references are from the ESV except where noted.

Becoming "And So" People

1   "Christ's Curate in Decapolis," The Spurgeon Center, https://www.spurgeon. org/resource-library/sermons/christs-curate-in-decapolis/#flipbook.

The Conquering Hero

1   John Calvin, *Calvin's Commentaries* (Michigan: Baker Book House, 1996), 16:214.
2   Ibid.

What Then Shall We Live By?

1   "Calvin's Commentary on Mark," Bible Hub, https://biblehub.com/ commentaries/calvin/mark/1.htm.

A Message at Just the Right Time

1   John Calvin, *Calvin's Commentaries*, 16:319.

His Call to Service

1   A. W. Tozer, *The Best of A. W. Tozer* (Michigan: Baker Book House, 1995), 2:87.

The Sabbath, Healing, and Teaching

1   "Matthew Henry's Commentary on Mark," Bible Study Tools, https://www. biblestudytools.com/commentaries/matthew-henry-complete/mark/1.html.

Prayer: Connecting with the Father

1   "Take Time to Be Holy by William Longstaff, 1882," Hymnary.org, https://hymnary.org/text/take_time_to_be_holy.

The Lord's Prayer: A Place in the Kingdom

1   "Only a Prayer Meeting," Spurgeongems.org, https://www.spurgeongems.org/chs_only-a-prayer-meeting.pdf.
2   "Interview with George Mueller," CCIOG.org, https://cciog.org/wp-content/uploads/2020/01/George-Mueller-The-Man-of-Faith-to-Whom-God-Gave-Millions-A.-Sims.pdf.
3   "The Preface to the Lord's Prayer," CCEL, https://ccel.org/ccel/watson/prayer.iii.html.
4   "Calvin's Commentary on Matthew," Bible Hub, https://biblehub.com/commentaries/calvin/matthew/6.htm.

The Lord's Prayer: A Role in the Kingdom

1   "Calvin's Commentary on Matthew."

The Lord's Prayer: An Obligation in the Kingdom

1   John Calvin, *Calvin's Commentaries*, 16:319.
2   "Matthew Henry's Commentary on Matthew," Bible Study Tools, https://www.biblestudytools.com/commentaries/matthew-henry-complete/matthew/6.html.

The Lord's Prayer: Provision

1   Jonathan Herron, "One Way Missionaries," https://www.jonathanherron.com/blog/one-way-missionaries-a-w-milne.

The Lord's Prayer: Redemption

1   John Calvin, *Calvin's Commentaries*, 16:330.

The Response of the Heart

1   "Sanctification," Gracegems.org, https://www.gracegems.org/Watson/sanctification.htm.
2   "Calvin's Institutes," CCEL, https://ccel.org/ccel/calvin/institutes.iv.iv.html.

What Do These Parables Say about How We Should Live?

1 "Sanctification," Gracegems.org, https://www.gracegems.org/Watson/sanctification.htm.

2 "Calvin's Institutes," CCEL, https://ccel.org/ccel/calvin/institutes.v.vii.html.

Let Your Light Shine

1 John Calvin, *Calvin's Commentaries*, 16:436.

Touching the Hem of His Garment

1 "The Touch," The Charles Spurgeon Sermon Collection, https://www.thekingdomcollective.com/spurgeon/sermon/1640.

2 Charles Spurgeon, *Miracles and Parables of Our Lord* (Michigan: Baker Book House, 2003), 2:299–300.

Believing in the Face of the Impossible

1 "Matthew Henry's Commentary on Mark."

Grace for the Journey

1 "Calvin's Commentary on Mark," Bible Hub, https://biblehub.com/commentaries/calvin/mark/6.htm.

The Lord Is My Shepherd

1 "Compassion for the Multitude," Spurgeongems.org, https://www.spurgeongems.org/sermon/chs453.pdf.

2 Ibid.

Things to Seek First

1 John Calvin, *Calvin's Commentaries*, 16:319.

Be Distinctive ... In Your Relationships

1 Dietrich Bonhoeffer, *The Cost of Discipleship* (New York: Simon and Schuster, 1995), 89.

2 "Spurgeon's Verse Expositions on John," Studylight.org, https://www.studylight.org/commentaries/eng/spe/john-12.html.

Be Distinctive ... In Your Work

1 Timothy Keller, *Gospel in Life* (Michigan: Zondervan, 2010).

Be Distinctive ... In Your Worship

1   "Christ and His Co-Workers," The Spurgeon Center, https://www.spurgeon. org/resource-library/sermons/christ-and-his-co-workers/#flipbook.

It is Better ...

1   Jerry Bridges, *The Practice of Godliness* (Colorado: NavPress, 2010), 96, 109.

Resting in Marriage

1   "Matthew Henry's Commentary on Ruth," Bible Hub, https://biblehub. com/commentaries/mhc/ruth/3.htm.

The Path of A Workman Approved

1   RC Sproul, *Knowing Scripture* (Illinois: InterVarsity Press, 1977), 23.

Printed in the United States
by Baker & Taylor Publisher Services